Beyond Christianity

Frank Parkinson

Evolution is a light that illuminates all things

Pierre Teilhard de Chardin

Ω
OMEGA
POINT PRESS

Copyright © Omega Point Press, 2020

Published in the UK by
Omega Point Press
14 Ryeheys Road
Lytham St Annes
Lancs. FY8 2HA

ISBN 978 1901482 027

Contents

Author's Preface

INTRODUCTION 1

Chapter 1 Relaying the Foundations 11
   A Parable for our Time 11
   The two great challenges 11

Chapter 2 Crisis in Christianity 13
   Two Revolutions, Two Revelations 13
   The Crisis in Scientific Belief 16
   Dividing the Garment of Truth 19
   Truth, Conscience and Flat-earth Theologies 21
   Is Truth Important? 23

Chapter 3 Christianity Evolving 29
   Gospel Fact, Gospel Fiction 29
   Resurrection: warrant or stumbling block? 35

Chapter 4 The Spiritual Quest 43
   What is spirituality? 43
   Spirituality and Mysticism 48
   Spirituality and Meditation 51
   Contemplation and Meditation 53

Chapter 5 The Rahner Paradox 59
   The need to know God 59
   Light from the East? 64
   The essence of Christianity 67

Chapter 6 Eckhartian revolution **71**
    Eckhart's vision of God 71
    Oneness: Orthodoxy or Heresy 74

Chapter 7 New Horizons **83**
    A new axial age 83
    A new creation story 86
    Neurotheology 91

Chapter 8 Seeking the Real "Me" **97**
    The evolving self 97
    The "I" that meets God 104

Chapter 9 The Evolution of God and Religion **111**
    From gods to God 111
    From theism to entheism 114

Chapter 10 Entheism and the Future of Religion **117**
    An outline of Entheism 117
    Entheism as cognition 120
    God in nature 124

Chapter 11 The New Good News **129**
    The new God-story 129
    Entheism as co-creation 131
    How realistic? 132

Chapter 12 Making the vision a reality **137**
    The passage to entheism 137
    The entheistic group 139
    From seed to fruit 142
    Looking into the future 146

Contents

Author's Preface

INTRODUCTION 1

Chapter 1 Relaying the Foundations 11
    A Parable for our Time 11
    The two great challenges 11

Chapter 2 Crisis in Christianity 13
    Two Revolutions, Two Revelations 13
    The Crisis in Scientific Belief 16
    Dividing the Garment of Truth 19
    Truth, Conscience and Flat-earth Theologies 21
    Is Truth Important? 23

Chapter 3 Christianity Evolving 29
    Gospel Fact, Gospel Fiction 29
    Resurrection: warrant or stumbling block? 35

Chapter 4 The Spiritual Quest 43
    What is spirituality? 43
    Spirituality and Mysticism 48
    Spirituality and Meditation 51
    Contemplation and Meditation 53

Chapter 5 The Rahner Paradox 59
    The need to know God 59
    Light from the East? 64
    The essence of Christianity 67

Chapter 6 Eckhartian revolution 71
Eckhart's vision of God 71
Oneness: Orthodoxy or Heresy 74

Chapter 7 New Horizons 83
A new axial age 83
A new creation story 86
Neurotheology 91

Chapter 8 Seeking the Real "Me" 97
The evolving self 97
The "I" that meets God 104

Chapter 9 The Evolution of God and Religion 111
From gods to God 111
From theism to entheism 114

Chapter 10 Entheism and the Future of Religion 117
An outline of Entheism 117
Entheism as cognition 120
God in nature 124

Chapter 11 The New Good News 129
The new God-story 129
Entheism as co-creation 131
How realistic? 132

Chapter 12 Making the vision a reality 137
The passage to entheism 137
The entheistic group 139
From seed to fruit 142
Looking into the future 146

Author's Preface

No individual could write authoritatively on a theme so vast as has been sketched here, but despite the manifest gaps and weaknesses in the present treatment the time has seemed right to make an attempt. As G. K. Chesterton put it, "If something is worth doing, it is worth doing badly," and the reader is asked to take that as a cover-all justification for short cuts in the argument and sometimes weakly supported generalisations.

More of the author's thoughts on science, religion and society can be found on the Internet

www.frankparkinson.co.uk

INTRODUCTION

In 2016 the Israeli scholar Yuval Noah Harari published *Sapiens: A Brief History of Humankind*. It rapidly became a best-seller, was translated into forty languages and reviewed in all the leading newspapers and literary magazines. It had clearly touched a nerve of some kind and *Beyond Christianity* aims to touch the same nerve but in a very different way. *Sapiens* was, as its subtitle implies, an essay in anthropology, bringing together a wide range of disciplines and showing the main historical forces which have converged to create the human species as we have it today. The critical reception was almost entirely positive, one reviewer calling it "a bible of mankind's cultural and economic and philosophical evolution [1]," but with some complaints about the lack of depth and detail in some areas. That weakness could be hardly avoided, however, in a historical survey which covered vast areas of science, politics, economics, religion, philosophy, ethics and zoology, to name only the most obvious, in its attempt to convince the reader that humankind, *Homo Sapiens*, is in existential crisis. The book's conclusion, in a nutshell, was that in our long evolutionary journey from animal to human the species *Homo Sapiens*, having brought meaning to the world is now evacuating it of meaning, more specifically of religious meaning. Harari's thesis is that through science we have wiped out the idea of God as the ultimate source of meaning and replaced it with a new quasi-religion of humanism. We have gone from a God-centred to a human-centred vision of reality in a Copernican shift. Specifically, Harari argues, we have invented an extra-human - and to that extent non-human - kind of consciousness in the form of artificial intelligence and robotics. This development increasingly dominates and orders our lives but in the process robs them of meaning unless we are prepared to consider willing slavery to these man-made but non-human systems a kind of meaning. More and more we live on what one reviewer wittily called "the planet of the apps." Harari ends the book and draws all the threads together with the following question: "What will happen to society, politics and daily life when non-conscious but highly intelligent algorithms know us better than we know ourselves?"

The answer to that question he provides in the equally popular sequel *Homo Deus: A Brief History of Tomorrow*. In this he introduces a second kind of religion, which he calls "Dataism", the point and purpose of which is somewhat obscure but which takes "information" to be both the new God and the greatest moral good. A major aim of Dataism is thus to increase information. This is certainly questionable, for there is a felt need today to diminish the flood of information that threatens to overwhelm us, numb our brains and diminish our decision-making capability. Rather, the great need today is finding a way to control and select from this tsunami of "data", most of which is trivial and much dehumanising. The concluding part of the book is taken up with speculation about where information technology is taking us and with this the overall pattern of the book is completed. The emergence of science and the invention of the computer are of particular significance in this Odyssey, the former because it has opened the way for technology, as well as doing away with the concept of God and in the process taking out of life what previously gave it meaning. The silicon chip has not only transformed communication, indeed almost redefined it, but has created trans-human, electromechanical entities, acting under instructions from algorithms, to which we increasingly subordinate our lives and, in so doing, diminish our value as individuals. Thus we become, though Harari does not emphasize the point, more herdlike in thought and behaviour, reversing evolution and taking us back towards the animal. He ends the book, to which he has already supplied a gloomy scenario, with the following question:

> *What will happen to society, politics and daily life when non-conscious but highly intelligent algorithms know us better than we know ourselves?*

In the mass these algorithms, which he does not define or categorise, come across as the brain of a new kind of Frankensteinian monster which *Homo sapiens* has created and over which it has lost control. With the advent of artificial intelligence and robotics we have in effect, created a new kind of consciousness embodied in self-assembling and quasi-creative machines and with it a new kind of will to which we have subordinated our normal human will. What kind of future human can be foreseen in this ominous development?

Sapiens and *Homo Deus* are by no means the only works which recognize that our species is now in a critical phase and which seek to look into the future to see where we might be going and assess the available options. In fact, Harari's two volumes [2] might be seen as representative of a new literary genre, a companion to science fiction, to which authors contribute different viewpoints on the human future and emphasize different aspects. The dystopian novels of George Orwell and Aldous Huxley are among the earliest and are certainly the best known exemplars of this growing body of futuristic writing [3].

Ray Kurzweil is probably the most optimistic, offering his belief that science will overcome all eventually. In line with this conviction, he has made arrangements for his body to be cryogenically preserved, to be resuscitated and rebuilt at some future time when the necessary theory and techniques have been invented [4]. The biologist and systems theorist Stuart Kauffman also puts his faith in science but in a different way, arguing that we must "reinvent the sacred in our secular world" but replace the perceived need for a creating power with a new theory of self-organising complexity [5]. Self-organisation and emergence have a suitably scientific ring and for that reason are the preferred solution for many scientists to the problem of creation. All that is needed is to substitute nature for God, sometimes capitalised as Nature and sometimes personalised as "she". In the words of the physicist Paul Davies,

> *An increasing number of scientists and writers have come to realize that the ability of the physical world to organize itself constitutes a fundamental, and deeply mysterious, property of the universe. The fact that nature has creative power .... challenges the very foundation of contemporary science.* [6]

Among the latest advocates for the pseudo-scientific theory of spontaneous creation is the celebrity physicist Professor Brian Cox whose *Human Universe* appeared in 2014, co-authored with Andrew Cohen, the head of the BBC Science Unit. It has much the same sweep as Harari's two works, the same faith in science as Kurzweil and settles like Kauffman for emergence as a vague answer to the questions "How?" and "Why?". Cox's approach, however, is unusual in that he ascribes a kind of objectivity to "meaning". For him it is "an emergent property [which] appeared on Earth when the brains of our ancestors became large enough to allow for primitive culture [7]." From this viewpoint what he sees is that "We humans represent an isolated island of meaning in a meaningless universe." He accepts that there may well be other civilisations elsewhere in our unimaginably vast universe, but so distant that there is no reasonable hope that *Homo sapiens* will ever be in communication with them. Our isolation in a world without purpose or meaning is complete. At the end of the book he defines the problem with a memorable epigram:

> *We've woken up at the wheel of the bus*
> *and realize we don't know how to drive it.*

With this conclusion the present work completely agrees and would emphasize that we are now confronting not a national or historical crisis but a species crisis: sapiens can no longer solve the global problems it has created and logic forces us therefore to the conclusion that a new kind of human, type or subspecies, is now called for. Its newness will come from the fact that it will have crossed a cognitive barrier. The new human will not only be more spiritually sensitive and God-aware - this being its defining property - but will also be more empathic, more highly developed intellectually, will have more logical power, and a greater store of information, thanks to information technology. This information will be organised largely on a historical axis, resulting in future humans thinking naturally in terms of past, present and a future that it knows it is helping to create.

Although *Beyond Christianity* may be classified within this new genre of books dealing with the human future, it is based on three premises which set it apart. Firstly, it assumes that "universe" must be defined differently since Hubble's discovery of the galactic redshift and its corollary that we live in an expanding universe. This has profound consequences not only for science but for religion. Proof that the cosmos came into existence at the moment we now know as the Big Bang implies that our three-dimensioned, time-bound cosmos is not the whole of scientific or theological reality and opens up a whole new creation. What once we thought was the whole universe is now revealed as a three-dimensional subspace of something else, from which it emerged at the instant of the Big Bang and to which it seems probable it will return, although that question is still open. This revelation - the word is not too strong - raises the following questions:
- Where did our world come from?
- How will it end?
- What is it expanding into?
- What force initiated and sustains this expansion?

Secondly, and relatedly, Beyond Christianity assumes that science, as a defined field of philosophy, evolves and there are many signs that a paradigm shift is imminent and overdue. It would be impossible to give a brief account of the gaps and anomalies in current science that are becoming ever more visible [8],but one thing is worth particular attention, namely, the inadequacies of naive Darwinism, which holds to a purely mechanical and deterministic model of natural selection as an act of faith and *modus operandi*. The whole argument is complex but is well summarized by the sociobiologist and Nobel Laureate E. O. Wilson in the following judgement:

> Homo Sapiens, *the first truly free species, is about to decommission natural selection, the force that made us ....*

> *Soon we must look deep within ourselves and decide what we wish to become* [9].

Wilson is an ardent opponent of religion, and rejects any idea of a divine power at work in the world, so his opinion echoes Harari's, that *Homo sapiens* has effectively elevated itself to be a god-substitute. More significantly, it opens the way for a theology of co-creation which is not to be found in the Christian creed or the teachings of any other religion. That is the main pillar of the present work.

The third premise on which *Beyond Christianity* is based is that Jesus of Nazareth is not a God come down from heaven above the clouds, although he may rightly be said to be divine in another sense. With modern knowledge of the nature of being human, he can more accurately and fruitfully be seen as a representative of a higher kind of human, manifesting an evolved consciousness which those of his generation were at a loss to categorise. We can say at the very least that it entails an exceptional sense of intimacy with the creating power, critically deeper than that which is experienced even by virtuous individuals. Its nature may be indicated for the present in the statement of Jesus in John's gospel, "the Father and I are one" (10:30). Whether or not he actually said this opens up critical questions about the reliability of the gospels as historical fact, which will be treated in Chapter two.

In postulating Jesus as an evolutionary forerunner *Beyond Christianity* breaks new ground in anthropology, implying that Jesus and similarly God-aware individuals who would today be classified as mystics, or of a mystical temperament, should be recognised as a distinct human type, rather than just simply exceptions to the norm. Professional anthropologists will find this assertion laughable, but if it is allowable to consider cavemen and modern humans as different types of the same species, there can be no objection in principle to sub-dividing *Homo Sapiens* on the basis of spiritual development. Biological anthropology, in the spirit of quantitative science, seeks always to distinguish by measuring and its standard benchmark for humanisation is brain size. However, while the fossil record shows increasing cranial capacity, what marks out man from other primates is unquestionably quality of consciousness, and this cannot be measured in any conventional way. How does one differentiate between Shakespeare and a chimpanzee? Perhaps a new kind of metric is now called for, but that is a problem not for scientists but for metascientists. In any event, if hominisation is co-extensive with spiritualisation, we are looking into a future where *Homo Sapiens Spiritualis* is accepted as a recognized type and Jesus is in this respect what biologists would call a holotype, that is, the first appearing specimen [10]. The question of labelling is important and it is of the greatest significance that Paul unambiguously refers to members of the newly founded movement of Christians as *Homo Novus*, that being a direct translation into Latin of his Greek term *kainos anthropos* (*Ephesians* 4:24), quite literally the "new human being". Furthermore he emphasizes the evolutionary significance of Jesus by calling him "the first born of a great new family" (*Romans* 8:29), which is to say, in more scientific terms, a holotype. The budding new humans might be given the biological classification *Homo Sapiens Christianus* but *Homo Novus* trips more easily off the tongue and makes clear that what is to come will be new and post-Christian, post-Islamic, post-Jewish or post any other religion. Members of this new type or subspecies would not only be dedicated to self-improvement, in a way that *Homo Sapiens* is not, but would strive to live habitually, as did Jesus, in the presence of the creating power and in awareness of doing its will. "Knowing God" as Jesus knew God would be the goal and purpose of life. The ambiguity in all this is, of course, that to the extent that Paul's great dream becomes a reality Jesus will no longer be unique, at least in the accepted sense. Rather, his uniqueness would be like that of the first person to climb Mount Everest or invent antibiotics. He would be seen as a trail-blazer. To accommodate this a new narrative or mythos will need to be constructed. However, it is unlikely that this reasoning will convince those who feel great psychological need for the traditional mythology that Jesus was, in the style of Greek drama, a God come down from heaven above, a real life *deus ex machina*.

In one very important respect, *Beyond Christianity* approaches spiritual evolution in a scientific and experimental spirit. It starts from the position that if one hypothesizes that communication with the creating power is possible and sets about establishing such communication with an agreed protocol, a change of consciousness can be predicted to happen. This change is something more than the *metanoia* of Christian doctrine, since it entails a fundamental change in habitual consciousness, variously labelled by such terms as "knowing God", "living in the presence", "the oneness" and intermittent periods of what has come to be called an altered state, when normal brain activity is suspended. The state itself is beyond words, and for that reason often called "mystical", but its nature may at least be initially indicated as the experience of a deep sense of the unity and rightness of things, of tranquillity and of absorption into a totally undefinable higher power. If this does not happen when a certain procedure or protocol has been followed, the experiment has failed and the hypothesis about divine-human communication has been falsified. However, the hypothesis may have failed because of the experimental procedure that has been adopted. Hence the religious truth-seeker's response should be to go back to the drawing board. The practical problem is that many such procedures are on offer, some mutually conflicting, some quite clearly no more than passing fads, and reliable guides are not easy to find. The present work will put forward suggestions which are time-tested and have a neurological basis.

The evolutionary dynamic of Christianity springs from the axiomatic belief that Jesus of Nazareth uniquely had the divine spirit within him, coupled with Paul's definition of his new religion as the quest to "have the mind that was in Christ Jesus" (*Philippians* 2:5-11). We can see now with the benefit of history that with this definition Paul not only planted the seeds of a new religion but of a new definition of religion. The logic that leads to this conclusion is obvious if to have Christ-consciousness by definition means having the same habitual sense of oneness with God as Jesus manifested. Without that awareness a Christian may be a follower and an imitator in an ethical sense - and that is challenge enough - but miss the essential significance of "Christ-consciousness". The so-called Apostles' Creed, which binds all Christian sects, contains no mention, or even a hint, of this *metanoia*. As for seeking oneness with the divine power, the life-changing challenge "to have the mind that was in Christ" in this critical respect has gone to the margin of Christianity and most Christians would regard it as an impossibility, and even as arrogance and delusion to seek for the same God-awareness that Jesus claimed and displayed.

We are now at a religious crossroads. Indeed, as the book will argue, we are facing an evolutionary barrier. We need to break free from credal Christianity, as Christianity broke free from Judaism and Judaism from the idol-worship of the neighbouring Semites. If the aim of Christianity really is to acquire Christ-consciousness in the radical sense just raised, the churches as presently constituted are simply not fit for purpose. The best they can do is to take us to the threshold. This harsh but inescapable conclusion stems from the fact that the defining principle of Christianity has become not *metanoia* in the fundamental and evolutionary sense intended by Paul but acceptance of the Christian myth, the word "myth" being used here in both a positive and negative sense. At a deep psychological level practising Christians feel that abandoning a pseudo-historical narrative, which is in many respects no more credible than *Cinderella* or *Gulliver's Travels*, would mean abandoning everything worthwhile in life. If, however, one takes another perspective and considers Jesus to have been a higher kind of human before his time, everything starts to fall into place. The consequence of seeing him as an evolutionary forerunner is truly dynamic, for one is then offered a clear choice, either to be a bystander in the great drama of human evolution or an active participant in taking it forward and, to that extent, a co-creator.

Notes and References

1. Tim Adams, in a review of the sequel, "*Homo Deus: A Brief History of Tomorrow* by Yuval Noah Harari review - chilling," The Guardian, 11.09.2016.
2. His later *21 Lessons for the 21st Century* (London: Vintage, 2018), completes what appears to be an unintended trilogy. It goes over much of the ground of the first two volumes, adding additional insight and emphasizing his personal answer to the global and species problems he has highlighted. His solution of two hours daily vipassana meditation has been dismissed as self-centred escapism by some critics but is at least a valuable starting point for debate.
3. Orwell and Huxley hardly need further reference, as their ideas and much of their invented terminology are now part of Western culture. George Orwell's dystopian novels, *Animal Farm* and *Nineteen Eighty-four*, were first published in 1945 and 1949 respectively, and Julian Huxley's *Brave New World* as early as 1932, when the terminal breakdown of society could already be foreseen. His later work *The Doors of Perception* (1954), dealing with drug-altered states as a way to experience the divine may be usefully compared with theme of the present book.
4. See Ray Kurzweil, *The Age of Spiritual Machines*. NY: Viking Penguin, 2000.
5. See Stuart Kauffman, *At Home in the Universe: The Search for the Laws of Self-Organization and Complexity*. NY: OUP, 1996.
6. Paul Davies, *The Cosmic Blueprint*. London: Penguin, 1995. p. 5.
7. Brian Cox and Andrew Cohen, *Human Universe*. London: Collins, 2015. p.5.
8. There is a growing number of books on this theme, mostly written by physicists, as the inadequacies of the current subatomic model become apparent. A good overall view is given in David Lindley, The End of Physics: The Myth of a Unified

Theory. London: Basic Books, 1995. A narrower treatment can be found in Peter Woit, Not Even Wrong: The Failure of String Theory and the Continuing Challenge to Unify the Laws of Physics, (London: Vintage Books, 2007) and Lee Smolin, *The Trouble with Physics: The Rise of String Theory, the Fall of a Science and What Comes Next.* (NY: Penguin: 2008).

9. E. O. Wilson, *Consilience: The Unity of Knowledge.* NY: (Random House, 1999. p. 5.)

10. This may be contested, since Hinduism had the concept of avatars, individuals in whom God was incarnated, several centuries before Christ, but it is poorly defined theologically and mixed up with a fanciful polytheism. Vishnu is usually, but by no means always, the divinity assumed to be incarnated in various saints and gurus.

CHAPTER 1
RELAYING THE FOUNDATIONS

A Parable for our Time

In a village in India lived a farmer who owned twenty five cows. When he died, and his will was read out, his three sons found that he had left all the cows to them, in the following proportions: one half to the eldest, then one third to the second son and one sixth to the youngest. This created a dilemma, since live cows were valuable, and no one wanted to cut up a cow, and besides, how could one decide what constituted exactly a sixth of a cow? They consulted the wise woman of the village, and she said she would resolve the problem for them, but her fee for this would be one cow. "A whole cow!" they all exclaimed in indignation, "That is far too much! Outrageous! Unthinkable!" "OK, then," she replied, "Work it out for yourselves, and come back to me, if you can't".

After puzzling over it for some days, they decided they would have to accept her offer, exorbitant as it seemed, and returned, bringing with them a cow for payment. "Tell us the secret," they asked, but she just walked off with her cow and, looking back over her shoulder, she said, "You can work it out for yourselves now."

Sure enough, she had solved it for them half of the 24 that remained was a neat 12, one third was 8 cows and a sixth was four - totalling 24. So they no longer had the messy responsibility of having to chop up a cow. Problem solved. Winners all round.

The two great challenges

The moral of the story may be put in the form of a question: what seemingly indispensable articles of orthodox Christian belief will have to be given up in order for everything else to start making sense in a post-scientific world, open up the way for a truly experiential religion and give meaning to life as the Christ-story once did and in so doing provided the basis for Western civilisation?

The two beliefs which will be seen to present the greatest challenges are the Bible account of human genesis and the bodily resurrection of Jesus. The latter touches upon the deepest nerve of belief and will be left for separate treatment later. The former is encapsulated in the story of our first parents, Adam and Eve, and the question that it poses today is simple and straightforward: is our species, *Homo sapiens*, descended from two perfect humans who deliberately disobeyed the God who had created them, and who passed on to their descendants the guilt from that primeval sin? Alternatively, are we descended from a lower animal form? Are we a fallen race of super-humans or, to use Disraeli's phrase, half way between ape and angel?

When the Bible was first written, the Adam story was as plausible a theory as any other to account for the fact that humans are a mix of good and bad tendencies, and the religious challenge could be explained in terms of recovering the state of perfection, which was the happy lot of our first parents. The theory of biological evolution has changed all that, however, for whatever its defects in the detail, it assures us that we are descended from apes and that fact completely changes the nature of the religious challenge. Christians cannot just pass over this by saying that the Adam story is a quaint way of accounting for the main fact that we have both good and bad traits, for in orthodox Christianity the significance of Jesus lies primarily in the fact that he gave his life on the cross to atone for our inherited guilt. Christianity as we know it pivots on the concept and reality of Original Sin. It is symbolically wiped out in baptism, as water is poured over the head of the recipient, usually a small child. Once the Adam story goes, a total reconstruction of Christianity is called for.

Replacing the Adam and Eve hypothesis with a broad evolutionary account of our human ancestry has the effect of turning our gaze from a mythical past to a future which will only come about as religious communities take on the task of building it. In this situation, the point and purpose of our existence will be clearly seen to be creating a higher kind of human. Co-creation will no longer be a new theological fashion but the meaning of our existence as humans and a here and now task for every individual.

CHAPTER 2
CRISIS IN CHRISTIANITY

The great Christian past, with its old majestic theme of man's fall and salvation, has collapsed. Rubble, broken arches, monuments crumbling to dust, roofs open to the sky litter this world of thought and loom forebodingly against the horizon ....
Can this litter of a dead past be cleared away?
Can man face the future with hope and with resolution without a sense of the past?
And if not, can a new past, truer than the old, be manufactured to give him a like confidence? These problems, I venture to suggest, lie at the very heart of our society.

J. H. Plumb, The Death of the Past [1]

Two Revolutions, Two Revelations

The theologies of all established religions have been made obsolete by two scientific discoveries in the past one hundred and fifty years. Both concern evolution and both constitute revelation in the most literal sense, for they reveal something about the way our universe and we as human beings have been created. Thus they reveal something of critical importance about the creating power which we have traditionally called God.

Both scientific discoveries are incomplete and thus, strictly, should be taken as theories rather than as facts, but the evidence that they are broadly correct is so overwhelming that they may be taken as factual truth. Both revelations have an immense bearing on the way we understand not only the creating power but the meaning of existence and the purpose of our own lives. Both discoveries are theologically dynamic, which is to say that in considering their full significance we are led towards a fundamental change in the way we think and feel about God and they initiate a change in our behaviour. Together these two scientific discoveries provide new spiritual energy, new incentive and capability to attain the goal of what the early Christian church called *metanoia* – change of consciousness.

The importance of these scientific revelations cannot be overstressed, for ultimately they must lead to a general awareness that the point of life is to develop into a new kind of human being, as different from what we now consider normal humanity as the normal human being today is different from our caveman ancestors. We can no longer be satisfied with the normal. In this regard it is worth quoting from the social psychologist R. D. Laing, who wrote in 1967, after two "wars to end all wars" had made the stark truth unavoidable:

> *Normal men have killed probably a hundred million of their fellow normal men in the last fifty years.* [2]

The logical consequence of this is that unless we redefine what is meant by "normal human being", we shall never escape the mindless inhumanity that has caused such violence, such destruction and loss of life. A new theology waiting to be born provides just such an escape: it offers salvation in the most literal sense. It is the introduction to a script for a new human future, and the prologue to a drama whose final act will be in effect the reinvention of the species. Those who would say that this is impossible, that human nature never changes, know nothing of our evolutionary history.

The first of these scientific/theological discoveries forcing us over a developmental barrier was Darwin's theory of biological evolution, which interpreted a range of evidence from nature and from the fossil record to show that species evolve, and the human species is part of this process. That is the simple, outline view: the details are complex and controversial. It is common to sum up Darwin's theory of human evolution in the snap phrase "Man came from monkeys", but the real significance of evolutionary theory comes not from looking back at what we once were but in looking forward to what we can be. As H. G. Wells put it a century ago:

> *The fact that man is not final is the great unmanageable, disturbing fact .... The question of what is to come after Homo sapiens is the most persistently fascinating and the most insoluble question in the whole world.* [3]

Darwin's scientific revelation forces us to make several theological decisions. Firstly, we must decide whether or not we believe that our species, and thus each individual, has further developmental potential and, secondly, unless the evidence leads us to believe that human evolution has suddenly and inexplicably come to an end, we must decide where it is heading and, more importantly, where we want it to go. For millions of years our species evolved blindly, under pressure of its environment like other species, but now we know that we can purposely change our environment and our nature, and this freedom brings with it an awesome responsibility: it forces upon us the question, what kind of humanity do we want to bring into existence? The Nobel laureate sociobiologist, E. O. Wilson, who is fiercely anti-religious, put it in a nutshell when he wrote,

> Homo sapiens, *the first truly free species, is about to decommission natural selection, the force that made us .... Soon we must look within ourselves and decide what we wish to become.* [4]

His words bring into sharp focus the rather hazy and romantic religious ideal of co-creation, increasingly used in religious circles. We find ourselves faced now with a theological and a practical challenge.

Various secular and religious ideals have been proposed in the past. Secular solutions have emphasized physical characteristics, such as Hitler's vision of a blond-haired Aryan master race or Soviet Communism's ideal of the hard-working Stakhanovite dedicated to the state. Religious solutions, by contrast, have emphasized a higher kind of consciousness, such as "the Buddha mind", "Krishna consciousness" and "Christ consciousness". Now we must ask are these religious concepts of the ideal human more or less equivalent and are they adequate to serve in the 21st century as models, or must we work out a new ideal, altering and adding to the old ones in order to take into account the fact that the great spiritual leaders of the past lived in a vastly different kind of world and thus had a limited consciousness. If what Buddhists call "the monkey mind" is at one end of the human evolutionary spectrum, what are we to aim for at the other end as humankind's goal? Whatever we decide will shape our evolutionary future. A radically new answer will ultimately produce a radically new kind of human being.

The second great scientific revelation came unexpectedly from the discovery by the astronomer Edwin Hubble and his collaborators in the 1920's that distant galaxies were emitting a reddish light, the so-called "galactic redshift". This observation led ultimately to the conclusion that they were moving away from each other. The scientific logic which led to this conclusion is not important here, for its significance arises from the wider conclusion that we live in an expanding universe. The revolution in scientific thinking which this discovery created is by no means yet over – indeed, it has hardly yet begun – and has had no impact on theology. It is all very new, so new, in fact, that Einstein's theories were originally based on the assumption that we live in a static universe composed of a single galaxy, our own Milky Way. Now we know that there are hundreds of billions of other galaxies, all moving away from each other at enormous speeds as space itself expands. At last count NASA put the number of galaxies at a staggering two trillion, each containing many billions of stars.

This is a staggeringly new view of the universe, and it faces both science and religion with two vital questions: how did it all begin and how will it eventually end? As regards the latter, there are two quite opposite conjectures so far - the Big Freeze and the Big Crunch. In the first case the expansion and cooling will come to an end as the temperature drops to absolute zero and, in the second, the build up of internal gravity as black holes proliferate, will start a contraction that will return the universe to its original point of unimaginable heat and energy. As the poet Robert Frost so neatly put it, "Some say the world will end in fire, some say in ice." There are actually other alternatives, but this thumbnail account will serve to show the magnificence of the cosmic drama on which Hubble drew back the curtain and the revolution in scientific thought that he set in train.

The Crisis in Scientific Belief

The scale of the revolution in astronomy set in train by Hubble and his associates becomes apparent when an imagined film of the expanding universe is wound back until we come to the first frame. Here there is scientific controversy which boils down to different acts of faith. On the one hand there are theorists who maintain that the universe began with a very small, but still finite, dense point of energy and on the other hand there are those who maintain that we must follow through the logic of "rewinding the film" to its end, which takes us to a seeming paradox, namely a point of no size, when, still winding our imaginary film, the whole vast cosmos will disappear, rather as the last dot of light on the screen disappeared when we switched off the old style television sets. This leads us to ask where will our familiar universe disappear to in this imaginary film, since this presumably is where it initially appeared from, and then to ask how, and why? Such questions are disconcerting to conventional scientists, who secretly wish they would go away. We have a finger-hold on the problem, however, in the fact that this dimensionless point has its counterpart in normal physics, which lives quite comfortably with the concept, and the reality, of the photon as a dimensionless point charge.

It is probably fair to say that belief in a cosmos which began as an immense point charge is not attractive to most physicists because it raises the seemingly theological question of where and how the point itself originated. It thus opens up the possibility of a creation event and, furthermore, represents a silent threat to conventional science, which is not equipped to deal with mathematical infinities or infinitesimals, for these are "non-objects", without size. Hence there is fear among scientists that to go further in exploring this new territory will lead straight back into the primitive religious pseudo-explanations from which science freed us four centuries ago. Robert Jastrow, the first chairman of the NASA moon exploration project, graphically expressed this fear in his 1978 book *God and the Astronomers*:

> *Theologians generally are delighted with the proof that the Universe had a beginning, but astronomers are curiously upset. .... It turns out that the scientist behaves the way the rest of us do when our beliefs are in conflict with the evidence. We become irritated, we pretend the conflict does not exist, or we paper it over with meaningless phrases .... For the scientist who has lived by his faith in the power of reason, the story [of modern cosmology] ends like a bad dream. He has scaled the mountains of ignorance, he is about to conquer the highest peak; as he pulls himself over the final rock, he is greeted by a band of theologians who have been sitting there for centuries.* [5]

What the scientists have found has become a subject of lively debate, with a tacit division along theological lines between those whose logic forces them to regard the Big Bang as an event which brought our three-dimensional world into existence from some prior reality and those whose logic equally prevents them from accepting the existence of any other kind of reality than the familiar world of our senses. Since it is almost universally assumed that time began at the moment of the Big Bang, and that any "prior reality" must be higher dimensioned, probably infinitely so, and timeless, it is not surprising that an emerging new science which deals with the timeless and infinite seems to many to be a contradiction in terms and no longer science as we understand it. Physics and cosmology are now at a critical threshold where what St Paul called "faith in things unseen" has become as important in science as in religion. What is vital in both cases, in order to distinguish such faith from gullibility, is to know the rational grounds for holding it and for building a science and religion upon it.

Scientific believers and non-believers both agree that the Big Bang, whether an exquisitely small point or a dimensionless geometrical point, consists of electromagnetic energy in an unimaginably dense state. This energy is made up ultimately of the same particles of light, photons, which not only enable us to see the world around us but make up the electrons, and thus the atoms of which we are composed. The Big Bang can be understood as originating in a single "super-photon" or "ur-photon", containing all the photons in the universe compressed, as it were, into one dimensionless point and this may be understood as the manifestation in three-dimensional space of a primal energy originating in a higher dimension. The consequence of this logic is that there must exist a source of energy beyond human sense, and this must be assumed as a premise in order to give logical cohesion to the Big Bang model. Such a "light beyond light" calls to mind the God of traditional Christian theology.

Science is undergoing crises at a fundamental level in other respects, not least in that its two fundamental theories of Einsteinian and quantum gravity are incompatible. Science's grand goal of a unified, overarching theory is therefore impossible. Either one or, most probably, both metatheories must be replaced or Science's grand goal of a unified, overarching theory is therefore impossible. If the deadlock is to be resolved, either one metatheory or, most probably both need to be replaced but this creates enormous difficulties, since almost everyone in science today has invested their career in the existing set of beliefs. The greatest crisis of all, however, comes from the fact that science has become detached from public understanding. This is particularly true as regards physics, which has become accessible only to mathematical specialists. There is now a need, almost a hunger, for a narrative science, which will tell the drama of science in a way that the ordinary person will find both understandable and logically satisfying. The outline of such a narrative will appear as the book's theme is advanced.

Without doubt the deepest crisis is not so much in science itself as within the scientific community and particularly in the biological sciences, where the neo-Darwinian thesis in its most generally accepted form leads to an apparent conflict between evidence and explanation that has become a matter of conscience. On the one hand, it is a sine qua non of the scientific method that magical forces or divine intervention are not allowable as explanations but, on the other hand, the principle of "natural selection" is manifestly inadequate to explain biological evolution except on a limited scale. Natural selection assumes that evolution has progressed by random genetic mutation which in conjunction with environmental factors has meant that only favourable genetic change has been passed on and become permanent in the struggle for survival. It is a satisfying mechanical explanation, which is the ideal of science, but it is an act of faith and in conflict with much of the evidence. The dilemma has been well put by a dedicated microbiologist:

> *The belief that the magnificent history of life is wholly the result of chance variation winnowed by selection for*

> short-term advantage has become almost an article of faith among biologists, but makes many others uncomfortable, and me also. Is this really all there is to "The Greatest Show on Earth" - no direction, no purpose, no goal and no meaning? Must we ultimately subscribe to the bleak assessment of the physicist Steven Weinberg, that "the more evolution is comprehensible, the more it also seems pointless?" I share the dislike for this conclusion, but the facts simply cannot be wished away. There is no evidence whatever for direction, goal or the guiding hand of a higher power. Moreover, given all that we have discovered, there is no obvious way in which any directive force could be brought to bear. [6]

This painful admission of honest agnosticism arises without doubt from the crisis in philosophy from which modern science was born in the 17th century when what were at the time called "natural philosophers" rejected pseudo-explanations through word analysis and "logic chopping" in favour of observable and repeatable evidence. It would hardly be an exaggeration to say that the new knowledge, nuova scienza, as Galileo called it, was promoted with religious fervour and produced its own martyrs until it overcame opposition and became a new orthodoxy. One unexpected consequence, however, has been that science has been forced to betray its own principles of honesty by ignoring counter-evidence to mechanical explanation. It continues to define "God" as the mythological entity once taken as an all-purpose explanation, along with devils and other spirits. There really is no conflict here once the scientist is prepared to admit ignorance and accept a category of "cause unknown". A simple "X-factor" pressed into service in appropriate cases, without invoking any of the religious or mythological assumptions of the God of religionists would retain scientific integrity. Indeed, the role of the scientist might then be seen to press research as far possible until this explanatory barrier is encountered. At this point the individual may decide whether or not he or she wishes to probe further into the God of religionists and, crucially, whether genuine communication with this God is possible or delusory. The nature of this conjectured communication is, perhaps surprisingly, a very live issue in religion and will be opened up in Part 3, "The Spiritual Quest" below.

Dividing the Garment of Truth

The great act of faith that scientists make today is a matter of negative belief that we cannot know how or why the Big Bang happened, but the great act of faith of "religionists" is also negative, that spiritual truth can only be conveyed through myth, legend, allegory and fable. In practice science and religion have agreed to partition truth into two territories, with observable and measurable truth being handed over to science and mythological truth to religion. The eminent palaeontologist Stephen Jay Gould formulated this as a principle, which he called, rather grandly, "Non-overlapping Magisteria of Authority" (or NOMA for short), meaning that science and religion could pursue their own kind of truth and need never interact. In fact, this was proposed eight centuries ago by the Moslem philosopher Averroes, and is known to philosophers as the Principle of the Double Truth. His followers, including many so-called Christian Averroists, held that it was morally acceptable to hold a religious truth in the religious compartment of one's mind, so to speak, and a contradictory truth in the scientific compartment. History is now repeating itself, for the great question then was the same one that confronts science today: has the universe existed forever, as taught by Aristotle, the "master" and by modern masters like the late Stephen Hawking, or was it created in time, as the Bible and the Koran teach. Hinduism and Buddhism offer a third option, that the creation of the universe is a cyclical event occurring over vast periods of time, but this does not avoid the question of how it came into being in the first place.

Many philosophers seized with relief on Averroes' get-out principle of two different but equally valid truth systems, for it sounds reasonable and apparently solved an insoluble problem of conscience. One outstanding theologian, however, led the movement against this comfortable pseudo-solution. Thomas Aquinas insisted that truth could not be divided in this way, and wrote his monumental *Summa Theologica* around 1250 to make his point by interpreting Christian theology in Aristotelian categories, which constituted the science of the time. Far from applauding his genius, the religious authorities on the whole were suspicious, and the archbishop of Paris went so far as to publicly burn Aquinas's books for trying to mix sacred theology with secular knowledge. In the end, however, the principle of the oneness of truth prevailed in the West, with the direct consequence that Islamic science which tacitly adopted the Principle of Double Truth, declined while western science, soon started to forge ahead. There is a great moral there for those who think we can have a healthy, truth-discovering science and religion by insulating each of them from the awkward questions that arise where their domains of enquiry overlap.

Although science and religion are both concerned with truth and reality, it is a sad fact that we rarely see them this way, for both are compromised. Science's honesty becomes dispensable as it becomes too closely associated with technological advance, big business and profit-making, and every religion's honesty becomes subordinated to propagating the particular myth on which it is based. "Truth simple" loses out every time to institutional truth. Religious leaders do not feel a primary responsibility to honesty and openness in matters of truth, for they take their calling to be to hand on a "deposit of faith" in which eternal truth is defined unquestioningly in terms of foundational myths, laid down in all cases in a pre-scientific age. Although minor myths can be reinterpreted without disturbing orthodoxy, questioning the great original myths is not allowed, it is heresy. All this is not to deny that spiritual understanding can be communicated through non-factual, essentially poetic, means. Nevertheless, the refusal of all mainstream religions to question, let alone abandon, their founding myths represents a kind of universal denialism. The hidden question is whether or not religion has come to the end of an evolutionary process which started with worship of the powers of nature – storm gods like Thor and Yahweh, fertility gods like Ceres and Baal and river gods, like the Ganges. There is, of course, no guarantee that human evolution will continue on an upward trajectory to a more intelligent and spiritually-minded species and, indeed, a survey of what is now happening in the world would suggest that regression rather than advance is more likely in the foreseeable future.

Truth, Conscience and Flat-earth Theologies

All the world's great religions are theories of reality proposed before it was generally known that we lived on a round earth, and this is almost certainly true of Jesus's world view. Hence it is not inaccurate to say that they are based quite literally on flat earth theologies. As a consequence, dedicated truth-seekers today are forced to believe very selectively in order to retain their intellectual integrity and must silently refuse assent to those items of belief that offend their commonsense. Many hang on in this way. There are sincere Jews who do not believe that a God above the clouds gave the land of Palestine to the tribe of Hebrews in perpetuity and ordered a genocidal slaughter of its original inhabitants [7], Catholics who do not believe that every Sunday they eat the real "body, blood, soul and divinity" of a God-man called Jesus, Protestants who do not believe in the literal truth of the Bible and Hindus who doubt that the cow is a specially sacred animal, though there is probably no practising Moslem who does not believe that all truth now and forever is revealed somewhere in the Koran. On that act of faith hinges both the strength and weakness of Islam, as with all religions based on closed-end revelation. Religion, like science, evolves, not only by incremental changes but by periodic upheavals, or paradigm shifts, when the grandeur of new revelation demands a re-laying of foundations. The mythological differences between so-called faith communities, would be a matter for mild humour, were it not for the fact that the world is likely to destroy itself as the cultural blocs, which have grown out of these ancient religious myths come into nuclear conflict. Those Christians who wish to harmonise religious myth, and scientific discovery tend only to spin pseudo-scientific fantasy mixed up with ancient myth, often elaborating on Teilhard's quite meaningless notion of the "cosmic Christ". Matthew Fox, for instance, the well known rebel Catholic priest and eco-theologian, redefines the Eucharist as "our eating and drinking of the Cosmic Christ [8]" and Karl Rahner loses touch with any semblance of reality, scientific or otherwise, as he proclaims, "When the vessel of his body was shattered in death, Christ was poured out over all the cosmos: he became actually, in his very humanity, what he had always been in his dignity, the innermost centre of creation [9]." This is but one of many examples of how irrational we can become in attempting to keep a foundational myth alive. Such myths are so bound up with the identity of the group and the self-identity of its individual members that they may almost be regarded as a kind of neural wiring. We do not so much believe in a cultural myth as live within it, thus rendering objective judgement about it almost impossible, insofar as we are totally unaware.

We take too much for granted that our particular religion, usually the one into which we were born and inducted without a decision on our part, is synonymous with truth. "Gospel truth" is a well worn phrase and a warranty, but as a historically reliable statement the expression is self-contradictory, for the gospels give clear evidence of textual changes made by unknown editors and copyists, who felt obliged to add their own insights or correct their predecessors' interpretation of many events. This fact, largely unknown to the average Bible reader, will be looked at in more detail in the section below "Gospel fact, gospel fiction". One particularly interesting anomaly arises from the fact that some early manuscripts of Luke's gospel portray Jesus praying on the cross, "Father, forgive them," but other manuscripts from about the same period make no mention of it. This raises a tricky question: did Jesus actually say these words and were they deleted by a Roman-hating Jewish scribe, or were they inserted by a scribe to drive home this most difficult teaching of Jesus, often referred to as the gospel of forgiveness? This is far from being scholarly quibbling. The revolutionary nature of Jesus's exhortation to forgive "not seven times but seventy times seven" is of the essence of the Christian message and the mark of a higher kind of human [10].

To complicate the situation, there is the indisputable fact that the mythical narrative of a "man of sorrows and acquainted with grief" who gave his life for the world is inspirational in a way that the factual account is not. The historical truth is that Jesus was executed by the Roman authority as a threat to civil order and the established power structure. Pontius Pilate, the Roman governor, was supported in his decision by the Jewish high priests, the Quislings of their time, for whom Jesus was also a threat, but crucifixion was a specific and public punishment meted out uniquely by Rome. The Jews never executed by crucifixion: their preferred method was stoning to death. It is ironic that what ignited and has driven the Christian revolution and created European civilisation is not the historical fact but the fiction image of a self-sacrificial god-man forgiving his executioners.

Is Truth Important?

Set against this background, the question *Is truth important?* is not so easy to answer as it may at first seem. Not all spiritual seekers feel the same need to know the factual truth and hence Christianity has become defined partly by acceptance of an ethical system as taught by Jesus and partly by belief in a complex myth centred on Jesus, which has spread and taken on a life of its own, with bizarre outgrowths. In the Roman Catholic version the mother of Jesus is taken up to heaven after her death to be reunited with her son, a fantasy that was promulgated infallibly by the pope as a new article of belief as recently as 1950. In the church calendar one can also find the feast days of St Joachim and St Anne, who, as invented parents of Mary the mother of God, could logically be called God's grandfather and grandmother, if Jesus is taken to be God in the literal and absolute sense that many take him to be. Despite all this, most practising Christians would probably agree with the sentiments of the former bishop of Oxford, John Harries, "I think the idea of a God who became incarnate and died upon the Cross and rose again, and who has our good in mind not just now but for eternity, is literally the most beautiful idea that has ever been thought of. Of course, because it is beautiful that doesn't mean to say it is bound to be true [11]." Similarly, Sri Aurobindo, an outstanding spiritual teacher and evolutionist, says in his *Essays on the Gita*, "It matters little whether or not a son of Mary physically lived and suffered and died in Judaea." The thrust of the present book is exactly the opposite: it matters critically now whether Jesus is taken to be a literal son of God come down from heaven temporarily to earth or whether he was essentially a new evolutionary type and thus a one-off in a limited sense and a blueprint for future generations. There is an urgent need now for the enduring essence of Christianity to be formulated in these terms, always bearing in mind that what made Jesus uniquely different from his contemporaries was his awareness of being "one with the Father" and experiencing the will of God as the meaning of existence and as a positive hunger (John 4:34). Understanding and sharing this experience of God is the great religious imperative of our time.

To dismiss the hunger for historical fact as a concern only for intellectuals would be completely to miss the point, for it is lack of historical credibility that is at the heart of the decay of the Christian story today. In society at large there is a general feeling, for instance, that the Christian story is from the past and on a level with nursery tales like *St George and the Dragon* or *Jack and the Beanstalk*. John Betjeman captures this feeling in his poem "Christmas" in the form of a question asked by a simple churchgoer. After some conventional and nostalgic verses about country churches, carols and lamplight, etc. he asks:

> *And is it true? And is it true,*
> *This most tremendous tale of all ...,*
> *The Maker of the stars and sea*
> *Became a child on earth for me?*

The most worrying fact of all is that many of those who preach the Jesus story do not themselves believe its most critical parts. A 2002 survey of 1,700 Anglican clergy by the polling organisation *Cost of Conscience* found that only 61 per cent believed in the bodily resurrection of Jesus and only 46 per cent in the, so-called, virgin birth [12]. These figures are not only cause for deepest concern but make one ask how these ministers can square their consciences with the very specific Thirty Nine Articles of Belief which once they took a vow to uphold.

Until a century or so ago most churchgoers in the West would have accepted unquestioningly the literal truth of the Christmas story, but no longer. Those who continue to accept it use the cover-all excuse that while the story may be in parts a fabrication, the important thing is that it is a myth and must not be taken as literal fact, since myth conveys a different kind of truth than do science or history. It is like poetry: it touches parts of our emotional brain that simple facts do not reach. This justification for clinging to the counter-factual and non-historical is no longer acceptable, and for two clear reasons. Firstly, it is arguably not possible to retain intellectual integrity while accepting a fiction in theology when the scientific and historical facts are available. Can someone be fully human if they cling to the Santa Claus story as an adult? Secondly, even if the case for myth-based truth be accepted, Christianity as currently structured does not on the whole offer spiritual seekers the experience of oneness with God which Jesus manifested and which is implicit in Paul's definition of Christianity as "having the mind that was in Christ Jesus" (*Philippians* 2:5, and elsewhere). In this respect the churches are not fit for purpose, for they make no claim to give their members the sense of oneness with a divine power that is the defining trait of Jesus.

The gospels say nothing of daily meditation as a way to what may be loosely called the experience of God, apart from a brief injunction not to babble words like the heathen but to pray in private and, presumably, silently (Matt. 6:7). However, the omission may not be significant, given the way in which the gospels were compiled, forty years or more after the death of Jesus, and largely by oral transmission from often hazy recollections. What is significant is that in the Christian tradition serious and systematic pursuit of Christ-consciousness has come to be regarded not as the heart of Christianity but as a special calling and separate structures have been set up to fulfil the needs of those who felt so called - dedicated communities of celibate monks, friars and nuns in the Catholic tradition and reform communities in the Protestant tradition, such as the Hutterites, Mennonites and Amish. For all practical purposes what Christianity offers is not attainment of Christ-consciousness but salvation from the guilt feelings of sin in this life and from an eternity in hell in the life to come. Opposed to this distorted theology now is an evolutionary Christ who was and still is a saviour but one who enables us to escape to a higher level of humanity and take on a new spiritual identity.

For lack of an evolutionary sense mainline Christianity is forced to stress inherited guilt in order to justify the saving virtue of a self-sacrificial God-man. The theory of Jesus the sacrificed saviour has become the very keystone of classical Christianity, and belief in its literal truth is explicit, as for example in the preamble to the Eucharistic prayer of the Church of England:

> *Almighty God, our heavenly father, who of thy tender mercy didst give thine only son Jesus Christ to suffer death upon the Cross for our redemption, who made there (by his oblation of himself one offered) a full, perfect and sufficient sacrifice, oblation and satisfaction for the sins of the whole world ....*

The same sentiments are found just as explicitly in the Roman Catholic Mass and in most Protestant worship, and they cannot be dismissed as antiquated expressions of a more subtle theology. The 1976 publication Christian Worship, a cooperative work of Baptists, Methodists and United Reform Church which was purposely written as an updating of "the eternal verities of God's revelation in Christ" finds nothing remarkable about including William Cowper's 18th century composition:

There is a fountain filled with blood
Drawn from Immanuel's veins;
And sinners plunged beneath that flood
Lose all their guilty stains ....

That, in a nutshell, is the grotesque myth and mindset that must be exorcised from Christianity if the core message of Jesus is to be retained and preached with new conviction. Other religions will have to abandon other myths if they are not to fossilize completely.

References

1. H. Plumb, *The Death of the Past*. London: Palgrave Macmillan, 2nd edn. 2004 [1969].
2. R. D. Laing, *The Politics of Experience*. Penguin, 1967. p. 24
3. H.G. Wells, from a lecture to the Royal Institute, reported in *Nature* 65:326-331, 1902.
4. E. O. Wilson, *Consilience: The Unity of Knowledge*. NY: Little Brown, 1999. p. 5.
5. Robert Jastrow, *God and the Astronomers*. London: W & W Norton, 1992 [1978], p. 107
6. Franklin M. Harold, *To Make the World Intelligible: A Scientist's Journey*. Victoria, BC, Canada: Friesent Press, 2016. p. 153. Harold is the author *The Way of the Cell: Molecules, Organisms and the Order of Life*. (Oxford UP, 2001) and *In Search of Cell History: The Evolution of Life's Building Blocks*. (Chicago UP, 2014).
7. As recounted in the book of Joshua and several places in the Old Testament, where God commands Moses, "In the cities of these nations whose land the Lord your God is giving you as a patrimony, do not leave any creature alive. Annihilate them all" (*Deuteronomy* 20:16). See also in the first Book of Samuel, "Do not spare them, kill men and women, children and infants" (15:2).

8. This is the central concept in Fox's futuristic theology of "Creation Spirituality", which is explicated at length in *The Coming of the Cosmic Christ* (NY: Bravo, 1990).
9. Quoted in Denis Edwards, *The God of Evolution: A Trinitarian Theology*. NY: Paulist Press, 199. p. 122.
10. Simon Wiesenthal, awarded a Nobel Peace Prize, and Elie Wiesel, both Holocaust survivors, offer deeply probing interpretations of an alternative, which Wiesel called "the Jewish doctrine of forgiveness". It centres on an obligation not to forgive when the problem of evil is as monstrous as in the Holocaust. Wiesenthal explores this in *The Sunflower: Possibilities and Limits of Forgiveness* (NY: Schocken, 1998 [1978]) with contributions from the Dalai Lama and other religious leaders.
11. In a much publicised debate with the arch-atheist Richard Dawkins at the Institute of Biology, Oxford on Feb 12th, 2009.
12. Cited in Hilary Wakeman, *Saving Christianity: New Thinking for Old Beliefs*. Dublin: The Liffey Press, 2003. p. 19.

CHAPTER 3
CHRISTIANITY EVOLVING

It is said in commendation of the famous scientist Louis Pasteur that he 'had the faith of a Breton peasant'. But while it is all very well for a Breton peasant to have the faith of a Breton peasant, it is not really praiseworthy for a modern scientist to hold the faith in the same manner. Modern science opens up vistas before us ... that are quite incompatible with the image of the cosmos traditional among Breton peasantry. To try to close one's eyes to these vistas is dishonest [and] betokens ingratitude of heart and pettiness of spirit.

Donald Nichol [1]

Gospel Fact, Gospel Fiction

It is commonly believed that Christianity was founded by Jesus and that the gospels represent an accurate historical account of his teaching and of his deeds. On both accounts there is serious misunderstanding and no progress in religion is possible until this has been corrected. It will be objected that it is not necessary to be a scholar to be spiritual or particularly intelligent in order to be a follower of Christ, and this is obviously true, but by the same token it is not necessary to belong to any religion in order to be a good human being; so we need to be clear why religion is of any importance at all. For a full understanding of the significance of Jesus in history and in one's spiritual development, a deeper knowledge of who he was and what he taught in the context of his times will be necessary.

It is clear that the contemporaries of Jesus regarded him as an outstanding individual. He was noticeably different, so much so that it was difficult to find a category in which to place him. The gospels recount several attempts to categorise him in order to understand his significance. Matthew's gospel (16:13-20) and similar passages in Mark and Luke summarises the situation, when Jesus asked his disciples, "Who do people say the Son of Man is"?

> They replied, "Some say John the Baptist, other Elijah and still others Jeremiah or one of the prophets. "But what about you?" he asked, "Who do you say I am?" Simon Peter answered, "You are the anointed one, the Son of the living God." Jesus replied, "Blessed are you, Simon son of

> *Jonah, you are a happy man, because ... revealed to you by my Father in heaven .... I will give you the keys of the kingdom of heaven; whatsoever you bind on earth will be considered also in heaven ...."*
>
> Matthew 16.18

This passage, coupled with belief that Peter was the first bishop of Rome, has been used to legitimate the claims of the Roman Catholic church that it was founded by Jesus and thus has a unique authority, but there is probably no scholar today who believes that this account is authentic. We know now, as previous ages did not, that it is a rewriting of history to provide blatant propaganda not for the religion which Jesus espoused but that which was initiated by Paul some years after the death of Jesus. It needs to be emphasized that Jesus himself wished only to reform Judaism and, at best, inaugurate a renewal movement for this purpose. At first he became a follower of John he Baptist, the main reformer at that time, and was baptized by him. We do not know why he then set up his own reform movement or indeed whether or not he also baptised like John, and the gospels are quite contradictory on this (See John 4: 1-2). As always, it must be borne in mind that the gospels were not written by eye witnesses and their intention was to promote Paul's Christianity as much as the high ethical doctrine of Jesus. After the death of Jesus, his core followers regrouped under the leadership of his brother James and later by other members of his family until it died out a century or so later, as did the Baptist movement. That James was the acknowledged leader is evidenced by the fact that it was he with whom Paul negotiated what was in effect a franchise, with regular payments "for the poor of Jerusalem" (1 Cor 16), ostensibly to spread the teachings of the Jesus movement outside Palestine. The reality was that this was an arrangement of convenience, enabling Paul to develop his new Jesus-centred religion among the gentiles, as well as sympathetic Jews, with minimum interference from Jerusalem and to create a quasi-official status for himself as "the apostle to the gentiles". Paul says explicitly that his religion came directly from Jesus himself in a moment of inspiration, thus giving him authority to preach it despite its originality: "I did not receive my gospel from any man, nor was I taught it, but received it by direct revelation from Jesus the Christ" (*Galatians* 1:12). The implication clearly is that he had had a vision in which Jesus spoke as the mouthpiece of God. It must always be kept in mind that Jesus himself explicitly forbade his message to be taken to the gentiles, which was exactly what Paul set out to do. "I was sent," Jesus said, "to the lost sheep of the House of Israel and to them alone" (*Matt* 15:4). The strength of his (initially surprising) abandonment of non-Jews is underlined by his repetition of this injunction in even stronger terms in the same gospel not to take his message to the gentiles and particularly not to the Samaritans (Matt 10:5) and, even more bluntly, not to cast the pearls of his wisdom before swine, as recounted in the Sermon on the Mount (Matt 7:6). The force of this prohibition cannot be fully appreciated if we do not know that the Samaritans were hated by Jews because they claimed to be in possession of the true Ark of the Covenant, which the Jews believed was in the temple at Jerusalem. Also, to get a true perspective on why Jesus excluded the gentiles from his mission, it is necessary to know that Jews routinely referred to gentiles as dogs and swine and, given the military occupation of Palestine by the gentile Romans. It would have made no sense for Jesus to have wanted his message of Jewish reform to be wasted on them. Seen in this light, the expression "casting pearls before swine" is far more than a striking metaphor.

As they stand, the gospels are a pastiche of fact and fiction and it will never be possible to reconstruct them to recover all the historical facts. We do not know who the authors are, and in fact there are certainly multiple authors, with each succeeding editor or copyist adding or subtracting facts and opinions as they thought best. Each was composed originally for a different community, compiled from handed down memories of Jesus, and because they were constantly being changed and added to in the early formative period it is impossible to date them with accuracy. However, scholars are now broadly agreed that the earliest gospel was written some forty years after Jesus died, giving ample opportunity for legends and anecdotes of various kinds to grow up and be incorporated in the Jesus story as historical facts. There is wide agreement that there was an early gospel, a sort of compendium of the sayings of Jesus, referred to as "Q", now lost, and that the synoptic gospels borrowed from this and from each other, to give something approaching a unified narrative. All four gospels reflect a different mix of Jewish and gentile readership and may be dated in a rough and ready chronology, as follows: Mark 70 AD, Matthew 80, Luke 90 and John 100. There are endless debates about dating, but these are probably close enough to the facts to be used as a practical marker and can be easily memorised.

We should not be too scandalized at the way in which the Christian scriptures were doctored by unknown editors and copyists, to the extent that they rewrote history. *Pseudepigrapha*, writing under another's name in order to give authority, was by no means confined to the gospel narratives. It was a widespread practice in the ancient world and in the case of Paul's epistles has had an ambiguous effect, in that it has both damaged and enhanced his doctrine. Some six of the thirteen epistles which bear his name are now considered to be inauthentic in whole or in part, with additions by unknown authors. On the negative side, one or more would-be "improvers" have made additions that blatantly contradict Paul's revolutionary moral teaching on social equality. This is summed up in the well known sentence in his *Epistle to the Galatians* (3:2) "There is no longer slave or freeman, male or female" (3:28), a ringing message which established his fledgling religion as an early proponent of gender equality. However in the later and almost certainly inauthentic *First Epistle to Timothy* he is made to say, "Women should remain silent in the assembly. They are not allowed to speak" (2:11-14). This and similar passages in other doubtfully authentic epistles conflict with evidence of the warmest relations that Paul clearly had with women, and which suggest that, far from being second class Christians, they were the backbone of his early church and it is likely that they will play a key role again as, and if, Christianity evolves from its current Nicene formulation. The later insertions and rewritings by male chauvinists, who could not accept the new social attitudes that Paul was preaching have, alas, given him an undeserved reputation for misogyny and made him a target for feminists. George Bernard Shaw went so far as to call Paul "the eternal enemy of Woman [2]", a snappy sound bite, but the opposite of the truth. In correcting, as they thought, this disturbing new doctrine of gender equality, the would-be improvers drove a coach and horses through an essential principle of Pauline Christianity, which subsequent generations of male priests have done nothing to correct. On the other hand, pseudepigrapha had positive effects, most notably perhaps in the *Epistle to the Ephesians*, which has been called the queen of the epistles. It is almost certainly not from Paul's hand, and not written in his style, but is a succinct expression of his vision of a community bound by mutual love and of Christians as being members of a new human type, creating "a single new humanity" in Christ (2:15). In this the unknown author may be said to amplify and give greater depth to Paul's teaching, as it has come down to us in his surviving letters.

Amid a swirl of fact and counter-fact two things stand out. The first is that the moral teaching of Jesus as reported is authentic and marks a step change in human evolution, a new definition of what it means to be human. We have lived with his innovations for so long that we have lost sight of how revolutionary they were at the time and indeed still are today. For instance, his so-called gospel of forgiveness was a clear moral advance on "an eye for an eye and a tooth for a tooth". What is rarely appreciated, however, is that the latter was itself a huge advance when it first appeared in Hammurabi's Babylonian code as far back as the eighteenth century BC. Although, thanks to Jesus, this injunction seems barbarous to us now, it was at the time an almost impossible moral demand, for the instinct of the "natural" human when offended would be to take unlimited revenge, if only to give a lesson to the aggressor. However much religion may change in the future, it is hard to see how Jesus' doctrine of forgiveness can be surpassed.

The second noteworthy element is that John's gospel, written two or three generations after the Pauline epistles is a systematic development of the sacrificial theology into which Paul fitted Jesus. There is no hesitation or ambiguity in John about the divine status of Jesus: he was the son of God come down from heaven and self-sacrificed for the sins of men. This would appeal to those brought up with Greek mythology, where gods and goddesses routinely travelled between heaven (located on Mount Olympus) and earth, but also to Jews who would have resonated with the concept of the scapegoat and the historical ritual in which all the sins of the tribe were symbolically loaded onto a scapegoat, which then was driven into the desert to die. The importance of this symbolic cleansing and forgiveness is recognized each year, in the great Jewish feast of Yom Kippur. In John's gospel this is subtly tweaked, so that Jesus is presented as a sacrificial lamb, rather than a goat. In general Paul's new religion is presented dramatically in John's gospel, almost as a series of pseudo-historical tableaux, and made to seem as if it originated with Jesus and thus had his authority. John's gospel has become almost a definitive statement of Christianity. How often do we see on notice boards outside Christian churches as a definitive statement of Christianity the sentence from John 3:16, "God so loved the world that he gave his one and only son, that whoever believes in him shall not perish but have eternal life."

The theory that Jesus pre-existed as God in a heaven above the clouds as part of a divine trinity and that he came down to earth effectively disguised as a human is known as Docetism, and despite the fact that it was officially classed as a heresy at the first Nicene Council in 325, it is largely the basis for what may be called popular Christianity. In its most common, and most misleading form, Docetism is expressed in the blunt statement, "Jesus is God", effectively making him an object of worship. The consequences of taking Jesus to be not a God-come-down-from-heaven but a higher and critically different type of human are profound. When they are spelled out, most individuals calling themselves Christian will at first find themselves at a loss and the objection will probably be raised that this is the ancient heresy of Arianism in an evolutionary guise. In this situation there will be a natural impulse to turn to authority and to what is taken to be the most reliable authority, the Christian scriptures. There is, however, no quick resolution available there, since almost everything in the gospels must be understood within the context of its time and establishing this context calls for a long period of study and reliable guides. The main historical axes are two indisputable facts, firstly, that Jesus was a Jew and his message was preached not as a new religion but as a refinement of Judaism, the unique superiority of which he never questioned. Secondly, Palestine, which in the national mythology had been given by Yahweh to the Jews, was at the time of Jesus occupied by Roman invaders, and thus every Jew had a moral obligation to drive them out. When Jesus talks about the "kingdom of God", there is usually this ambiguity: is he referring to the reign of God in the human heart, or the very practical problem of ridding Palestine, God's Holy Land, of the Roman pagans? What he and John the Baptist preached was that God would not expel the Roman invaders until the Jews had "repented of sin", thus fulfilling the contract that Yahweh had made with Abraham and Moses.

Jesus lived in one of the most fascinating periods in Jewish history, with two totally different solutions to the problem of foreign occupation proposed, namely military insurrection and moral reform. The assumption behind the latter was that repentance from sin would persuade God to intervene on behalf of his chosen people. The military option had already been tried in the late Greek empire and had been successful under the leadership of the Maccabee family, who had seemingly proved that religious zeal was sufficient for little Israel to overcome the greatest imperial opponent. Reassured by the success of their revolt in 166 BC, there were continual attempts at rebellion when the Romans displaced the Greeks and occupied Palestine about a century later. One notable attempt was by Judas of Galilee, around 6 AD, which ended with his crucifixion and that of hundreds of his followers. This would surely have left a great impression on Jesus, who would have been a small boy at the time. Rebellion broke out again in 66 and 132, when the Romans ended this continual threat of insurrection by destroying Jerusalem and dispersing its inhabitants.

These sketchy historical details are given no mention in the Christian scriptures and yet they are critical in determining what Jesus stood for. The Jesus story was rewritten to make it acceptable to non-Jews, notoriously so in absolving the Romans of blame for his death, as summarised in the enduring image of Pontius Pilate washing his hands of the matter. To do this, history was rewritten in the gospels of Mark (15:13) and Luke (23:21) in which the Jewish mob are represented as shouting, "Crucify him!" This falsehood has resulted in untold persecution of the Jews through the centuries on the grounds that they were God-killers. This is only one of innumerable instances where the gospel narrative needs to be corrected by reference to historical scholarship and, fortunately, there are many popular works where the main findings have been made available to a general readership [3]. The problem is that in trying to find the facts, many of which can never be anything more than probabilities, one is confronted with a mass of evidence and opinion, leaving the truth seeker, like a juror in a serious fraud case, quite overwhelmed by facts, often contradictory, and a plethora of unprovable suppositions. A serious course of reading in this field, and discussion where possible, is now a necessity for anyone who wishes to know who Jesus was, what he did, what he taught and his significance for our time. The magnetic north to guide the seeker through all the uncertainties is the realisation that none of the gospel writers ever set out to write history in the modern sense as neutral observers: their aim was to tell a gripping story, shape certain key events in the life of Jesus and, if necessary, invent them in order to convince readers that Jesus was a truly divine human and in this they have been for nearly two thousand years eminently successful.

Resurrection: warrant or stumbling block?

As one goes down this path, the divergence that appears between the traditional Christian story and the historical facts is likely at first to induce a sense of disorientation. The greatest psychological obstacle to acceptance of the evolutionary Jesus will arise when a decision must be made to include or exclude the Resurrection from the Christian narrative, for the literal truth of its happening is the theological keystone holding together the whole arch of credal Christianity. Even to question the literal truth of the Resurrection will be unthinkable for most church-going Christians, who simply will not be able to imagine that so many millions of spiritual and highly intelligent people throughout the centuries could have been mistaken. Two things must be kept in mind for a reasoned judgement to be made. Firstly, until the last century or so, the critical historical evidence was not available, and to break ranks with the consensus would have been to cut oneself off from society. It must also be remembered that the level of secular understanding of our world was far lower then than it is today. Until five centuries ago the finest brains believed that the earth was the centre of the universe and babies were born from male sperm, each of which was an invisibly minute human, a *homunculus*, complete in every detail, which only needed to grow to maturity in the mother's womb. At the time such speculation was by no means unreasonable, and so too many of the quasi-historical facts in the Bible. Secondly, and most critically, the gospel narrative, including the epistles and Luke's *Acts of the Apostles*, constitute a theory of history and of ultimate reality, and thus form a framework of understanding within which almost everything in life has been interpreted for nearly two thousand years, in the West at least. From it has come society's "intuitive" judgement of what is right and wrong, systems of education, of politics, of law, of sexual behaviour and commercial dealing. It needs little imagination to understand what a huge vacuum must appear in society and in the individual's approach to living as this framework crumbles and disappears. The times call for intellectual and moral courage and, most of all, for a systematic re-education.

There have been hundreds of books and articles written for and against the authenticity of the bodily Resurrection of Jesus – that his spirit lives on is not in question – and unravelling the doctrine and how it came into existence is a complex and demanding task. Three simple points may be selected here, however, to give a first indication that a literal Resurrection never happened. Before listing them, it should be emphasized that the decisive act of "un-belief" will be traumatic, perhaps almost unbearably so, even for many who may be convinced intellectually. The question asked above: "Is Truth Important?" will then suddenly take on a new relevance. With that in mind the following points are put forward.

The earliest gospels, Mark and Matthew, mention the Resurrection in no more than a couple of paragraphs and then end abruptly. Given that the Resurrection plays so pivotal a part in Christian doctrine, the minimal mention in the early gospels, half a page out of fifty, strongly suggests that it was a later addition, when the Resurrection myth had become part of common teaching. As evidence against its factuality, it falls into the category of "the dog that didn't bark", for if Jesus really did rise from the dead and if this fact was so central to the religion of Christianity, such a brief mention and abrupt ending would be as unlikely as a biography of Christopher Columbus which noted in the last couple of pages, almost as an afterthought, that he had discovered America. A second oblique piece of evidence against the historical reality of the Resurrection may be seen in the fact that Matthew's gospel mentions other resurrections as historical facts to which no one would give the slightest credence today. It recounts that at the moment when Jesus died, "there was an earthquake, the rocks split and the graves opened, and many of God's saints were raised from sleep, and coming out of their graves ... they entered the Holy City, where many saw them" (27:50-53). One might reasonably ask where they went thereafter, but the main point is that if Christianity is concerned with truth and honesty, one must ask why believe the gospel account of one resurrection but smile at the naivety of the other? The elephant in the theological room, however, is the general ignoring of the fact that Paul preached the resurrection of Jesus as part of a wider and wilder theory of a general resurrection of all Christians, which he predicted, was quite imminent but did not happen. In his First Epistle to the Thessalonians, which is generally accepted as authentic, he wrote:

> *For the Lord himself, with a cry of command, with the archangel's call and with the sound of God's trumpet, will descend from heaven, and the dead in Christ will rise first. Then we who are alive, who are left, will be caught up in the clouds together with them to meet the Lord in the air; and so we will be with the Lord forever. Therefore encourage each other with these words. (4:16-17).*

That is surely one of the most astonishing passages in the whole of the Bible. No reasonable person could accept its argument today, although some Christian sects, especially in America, persuade themselves that Paul only got the timing wrong and await the second coming, otherwise called "the Rapture", in their lifetime, or soon after. If the general resurrection of dead Christians is rejected as an imaginative attempt by Paul to demonstrate the uniqueness and spiritual power of Jesus to a mostly illiterate and more credulous audience than today, there is no reason to accept as historical the specific resurrection of Jesus. One of the most interesting facts in this debate, is that Paul freely admits that he will go to any lengths to spread his gospel, so important does he feel it to be. He describes himself by the unusual term *panourgos* (2 Cor 12:16) which has a most pejorative denotation, meaning "willing to use any means". Greek-English dictionaries translate it with words like "cunning", "crafty" and "unscrupulous". To invent a fictitious resurrection is not so dishonest as may at first seem, given that other examples can be found in the New Testament, such as the raising of Lazarus and the son of the Widow of Nain and, similarly with the Ascension, which is no more and no less miraculous than the transport to heaven of Elijah in a famous chariot of fire.

Arguments for and against a literal resurrection and return may go on forever but in the end the only question worth discussing is, what would be lost of the essence of Christianity if Jesus did not rise from the dead? Until very recently the historical truth of the gospels had to be taken broadly as a given, despite glaring anomalies such as the Second Coming, for there was hardly any factual record against which it could be measured. Not the least of these anomalies is the order given by Jesus to his twelve apostles not to preach his message to non-Jews, quoted above, which he flatly contradicts later in the same gospel with, "Go to all nations and make disciples of them, baptizing them in the name of the Father, Son and Holy Spirit"(Matt 28;19). Did he have a sudden insight which made him change his mind? This is most unlikely, and the obvious interpretation is that the first instruction was what Jesus actually said, or something close to it, while the second was invented by some unknown editor after Paul's universal post-Jewish religion had taken root. Once in the text it would be copied thereafter and eventually become canonical and a part of gospel truth. Things are now changing, however, and at an unprecedented speed. With the discovery of the Dead Sea and Nag Hammadi documents and an accumulation of contextual clues from archaeology, linguistics and comparative religion, it is now possible to draw firmer conclusions about what Jesus actually said or did, and they are startling. The seventy-odd scholars of the 'Jesus Seminar' are in agreement that less than five per cent of the sayings of Jesus in John's gospel have any basis in historical fact. They are in effect Paul's doctrine for the gentiles put into the mouth of Jesus. Such findings have created an existential crisis in Christianity.

Promise of eternal life was, and still is, the great selling point of Christianity. Christian funeral services commonly centre on the gospel declaration of Jesus (almost certainly put into his mouth by the evangelist), "I am the resurrection and the life: whoever believes in me will never die." This was something new to Judaism, which, doubtless as a reaction to the Egyptian cult of death and mummification, takes no definite position on an afterlife. The Sadducees, representing official Judaism, held that there was none, thus making Judaism a very here and now religion, with material reward in this life for living righteously and keeping to the contract with God. The sect of the Pharisees, which originated as a reforming movement, believed that there would be a resurrection of the dead at some future time but offered no details. In *Acts* (23:6) Paul described himself as a Pharisee and the son of Pharisees, and this is surely significant, given that rising from the dead plays so great a part in both Pharisaism and Paul's version of Christianity. In this new religion Jesus was the first of those to rise from the dead and thus both a promise and proof, of a sort. Paul raises the theological stakes in a way that is almost moral blackmail by specifically demanding that his followers believe in a literal raising from the dead. He presents his case, like a lawyer, in the fifteenth chapter of his first letter to the Corinthians, but when read with attention his logic is seen to be hardly more than bluster, as he switches between real, physical bodies and a confusing category of "spiritual bodies" which he invents for the purpose.

As so often happens in real life, telling one untruth ends up with a need to invent others to support it, and with the Resurrection story came the problem of how to dispose of a body that cannot die in the normal way. To resolve this dilemma the Christos myth started to take on a life of its own with the supporting story of the Ascension. That it clearly is a later invention is borne out by the fact that it does not appear in the gospels of Matthew, Mark and Luke and is an obvious addition in John, necessitating the additional fiction of Jesus promising his disciples to return to earth. Over all this theological debate looms a second great question: can a religion without a literal Resurrection still be called Christianity? In rejecting it, would one be losing something vital, of the essence?

The accumulating evidence that the Christ story is mostly non-historical generates strong emotions as it is brought under scrutiny. Most thoughtful Christians, as they become aware of the contradictions between historical fact and the gospel narrative, probably seek to resolve them by accepting the anomalies but claiming that they do not overall affect the truth of the gospels, however it is hard to dismiss such disturbing passages in the gospels as when Jesus, revered as "the Prince of Peace", supposedly said, "Bring here those enemies of mine who did not want me to be king over them and slay them right here in front of me" (Luke 19:27) or when he tells his followers, "If you don't have a sword, sell your cloak and buy one" (Luke 22:36) [4]. It is easy to accept that the true narrative has been doctored in these and other obvious instances. However, once that has been conceded, the authenticity of everything is called into question and one is forced into a situation where one must choose to believe this but not that, largely through intuition, thus in effect writing one's own gospel. Scriptural scholars are notoriously selective, as a few brief quotes will illustrate. John Macquarrie says that "the birth narratives ... are manifestly legendary in character." Raymond E. Brown, an authoritative Catholic scholar and a recognized conservative, has to admit that "the biblical evidence leaves the question of the virginal conception (more commonly termed the Virgin Birth) unresolved." John Polkinghorne, professor of physics and ordained Anglican minister, accepts the virginal conception as a credible option but dismisses the Ascension as "quaint" and altogether too naïve for the modern mind. He does not, however, note that if a bodily ascension is ruled out, the Christian must find another way of ending the story of a resurrected Jesus. Canon Arthur Peacocke, winner of the prestigious Templeton Prize for progress in science and religion had no difficulty in declaring that science puts paid to both the Virgin Birth and the Ascension but cannot be called upon in the search for truth in the case of the Resurrection, because the New Testament story "can properly be claimed to be referring to a new kind of reality, hitherto unknown ... on which science as such can make no comment [5]." If religious seekers after truth today are true to their conscience, they must ask what specifically is it about this "new kind of reality" that puts the Resurrection beyond the bounds of normal historical enquiry. David Jenkins, when Bishop of Durham, notoriously questioned the Resurrection, saying that it was "not a single event but a series of experiences that gradually convinced people that Jesus's life, power, purpose and personality were still continuing" and that is probably close to the truth, but is in conflict with what Christians must believe and which defines them as Christians.

As the streams of new discoveries converge, they strengthen understanding of Jesus as a turning point in evolution, and as the view from this new perspective becomes clearer, it forces a massively difficult choice upon the churches, a choice that may be compared to that which faced Jewish converts to Paul's vision of a trinitarian God, for they could not accept this without rejecting essential elements of their native Judaism. The natural response of Jews to the Jesus phenomenon, if one may so put it, was that he was an exceptional prophet, a new Elijah, and perhaps a new David who would throw off the Roman yoke, as the first David overcame the Philistines, who were contending with the Israelites for the land of Palestine. Those Jews who became followers of Paul, and thus believers in his 'Father-Son-Spirit' God, had to start on building a quite new relationship with a previously distant God, essentially a dialogue with God the Holy Spirit. For a Jew this spiritual intimacy must have been difficult to comprehend. To some it would have come as a threat to a once secure, orthodox and understandable way of religion, almost a heresy, to others as a marvellous new spiritual opportunity, with consequences to be explored. As will be seen, Eckhart's theology was later to offer Christians an even more intimate relationship, too intimate for the Church authorities, and this too was condemned as heresy. Paul at first played down the conflict of belief and in dubbing himself the apostle to the gentiles created ambiguity about whether his converts were primarily reformed Jews or members of his new religion of salvation. This no doubt strategic deception could not last and in 83 AD the break was officially made. Those Jews who counted themselves as followers of Jesus in the Pauline way - i.e., regarding him as the saviour of the world - were ejected from the synagogues, ritually cursed and their expulsion sealed with a mock burial service: they were now considered dead by their fellow Jews. After that there could be no escaping the choice, with all its pain, between staying a Jew or rejecting the religion of one's birth to become a Christian.

A similar situation will eventually arise for thoughtful Christians, whether to follow a real or half-mythical Jesus. Choosing the former brings with it a commitment to spiritual transformation that most nominal Christians will no doubt consider quite 'over the top' and it is hard to see how in the long term a break with the official churches can be avoided, as Christianity, supposedly founded by Jesus, had to break away from the religion he loved and for which he gave his life. There is a striking parallel between a new kind of religion struggling to be born today within its parent Christianity and the struggle of Pauline Christianity within its parent Judaism. Although Christianity took with it the Jewish scriptures and much of its moral teaching, it was clearly no longer a Jewish sect and a clear break and a fresh start were required - new structures of authority, new learning material, new modes of behaviour. Today, as the vitality and inspiration of credal Christianity ebbs away, we find ourselves in a very similar situation to that of Paul's first Jewish converts. Creating these new religious forms will constitute a long and detailed task, beyond the scope of the present introductory work. It is notable that Paul regarded the logistics of community building and governance (*kyberneseis* - 1 Cor. 12:27) as a charism and a particular gift of the Spirit. That gift will be needed in its fullest measure, if what might be called the essence of Christianity is to be identified and transmitted in a form that will inspire the modern age and generate the same excitement as that which is so vividly recorded in the *Acts of the Apostles*.

Notes and References

1. Donald Nichol, *Holiness*. London: Darton, Longman and Todd, 1981. 4th edn. 2004. p. 14.
2. Quoted in Calvin J. Roetzel, *The Letters of Paul: Conversations in Context*. KY: Louisville, Westminster John Knox Press, 1974, 4th edn., 1998. p.182.
3. The breadth and depth of literature on the historicity of the scriptures presents a problem for those coming to the search for the first time. There is always a danger of being overwhelmed by the piling up of scholarly detail. The following titles are more or less graded in terms of difficulty for the uninitiated, but even the most

simplified will call for serious application. There is considerable overlap between them, but the different viewpoints combine to build up a depth of understanding.

Albert Nolan, *Jesus Before Christianity* (Darton, Longman and Todd, 1977). This has gone through more than a dozen reprintings and is somewhat dated now, but was praised by Harvey Cox as "the most accurate and balanced short reconstruction of the life of the historical Jesus." John Shelby Spong, *Liberating the Gospels: Reading the Bible Through Jewish Eyes* (San Francisco: Harper, 1996). Contains a surprising amount of scholarly detail made palatable by a fluent writing style.

Russell Shorto, *Gospel Truth: The New Image of Jesus Emerging from Science and History and Why it Matters*. (London: Hodder & Stoughton, 1997). Written by a journalist but one who has done his homework and writes in an engaging style.

Bart D. Ehrman, *Misquoting Jesus: The Story Behind Who Changed the Bible and Why* (San Franciso: Harper, 2005). One of several books on related themes by an excellent scholar, and a best seller.

Burton L Mack, *Who Wrote the New Testament: The Making of the Christian Myth* (San Francisco: Harper, 1989). A somewhat denser but rewarding treatment of the general theme.

4. This is unlikely to be attributable to Jesus, although there is evidence that his close followers included those who favoured a military solution to Roman occupation. The evidence for this hypothesis has been put forward in detail by Robert Eisenman in *James the Brother of Jesus: The Key to Unlocking the Secrets of Early Christianity and the Dead Sea Scrolls*. (NY: Viking, 1997). On this assumption, it is probable that the injunction to buy swords was inserted in an early gospel document when the spiritual solution was perceived as a failure after the death of Jesus.

5. Citations in order from: John Macquarrie, *Jesus Christ in Modern Thought* (London: SCM, 1990), p. 192). Raymond E Brown, *The Birth of the Messiah* (London: Chapman, 1977), p. 527). John Polkinghorne, *Science and Christian Belief*. (London: SPCK, 1997 [1994], p. 121. Arthur Peacocke, *God and Science: A Quest for Christian Credibility*. (London: SCM, 1996), p. 77. The 1984 quotation from David Jenkins is from the Wikipedia entry.

CHAPTER 4
THE SPIRITUAL QUEST

The time is propitious for the discovery of a universal spirituality. To this end, not dogmatic religion but mystical and poetic vision is needed to release the potentials of spirit in an increasingly secular society. [It will be] existential rather than credal ... intensely intimate and transformative.

David Tacey, *The Spirituality Revolution* [1]

What is spirituality?

Augustine says somewhere that everyone knows what time is until they are asked to define it, and much the same can be said about spirituality. The word originated in Christianity, referring to the transformative role of God the Holy Spirit in human affairs, but is used today most frequently without religious connotation and indeed often opposed to religion. As the West becomes more secularised, a feeling grows, and is often expressed, that religion is bad but spirituality is good. Religion is authoritarian and guilt-inducing, while spirituality is liberating and ennobling. If asked, many people will say, proudly or defensively, that they are spiritual but not religious. The root meaning of spirituality is "breath" (as in "respiration"), which suggests something insubstantial, formless and immeasurable but having the power to enliven or move things, like a wind. In the New Testament account of Pentecost the Spirit of God makes its presence felt as a "rushing wind" and as "parted tongues of fire" (Acts 2:3), powerful symbols of God as a life-giving power and as a source of spiritual energy. This is the new understanding of God that the author wished to communicate and it marks a clear break with religion based on worship of a distant Creator-God. The Holy Spirit is at the core of Christian theology but in other religions it is peripheral, or non-existent, notably in Islam. Paul punches out the new understanding in his second letter to the Corinthians:

> *What I am telling you is not in words acquired through human wisdom but in words taught by the Spirit. I am explaining spiritual realities with Spirit-taught words.* (2 Cor. 2:13).

Its importance in Christianity may be gauged from the fact that Jesus, supposedly, said that to argue against the existence of the Holy Spirit is the only unforgivable sin (Mark 3: 28-30). It is highly unlikely however that Jesus would actually have said this, for there is nothing in the God of the Jews about God-within, whereas Paul's elevation of Jesus to divine status forced the concept of God-as-Spirit into existence as a link between divine and human. Jesus associated himself with it when he promised that after he had left this earth his message would be continued by the same divine Spirit by which he was himself inspired: "The Advocate, the Holy Spirit, whom the Father will send in my name, will teach you all things and remind you of everything I have said to you" (John 14:26). Again, however, we need to remind ourselves that the Trinitarian model of God was Paul's invention and the gospels, especially John's, were written in their final form to make it seem as if it originated with Jesus. There is no indication that the followers of Jesus who came together after his death under the leadership of James his younger brother preached anything other than a reformed Judaism, continuing the mission of Jesus.

The doctrine of a triune God defines both a new understanding of the Ultimate Reality and a new definition of what it means to be fully human, which might now be described as 'Spirit-inspired' and 'Spirit-motivated'. As the implications of being "fully human" in this sense are explored, there grows a sense that it entails something other than being human, as normally understood, but it takes time to come into full awareness of what is involved. One might see it in terms of leaving behind the familiar self-centred "me" and transforming into a God-centred me or, differently expressed, consenting to a take-over of one's conscious life by a higher power. From this new angle of vision we are not so much bodies containing a soul as the manifestation of a Spirit which has taken bodily form in each of us as individuals and corporately as a Spirit-aware community, which Paul called "the body of Christ" (1 Cor 12:27). Christ-consciousness is assumed to be the highest possible intellectual and emotional human development and acquiring it will involve a journey, knowing little of the goal as we start on it, what it will demand or what effects it will have on us. For a long period it will mean having a divided personality with two selves within struggling for dominance, for such a transformation of self cannot happen all at once.

To become *what I know I ought to be* I must abandon *what I am*. This is, we may presume, what Jesus was talking about in the parable of the pearl of great price: "The Kingdom of Heaven is like a merchant looking for top quality pearls, who found one of unique beauty, with a price to match, and sold all the pearls he had in order to buy it" (Matthew 13: 45-46). The "Kingdom of Heaven" is doubtless a metaphor for knowing God in a deeper way, not by comprehension, the root meaning of which is "grasping". As all the great spiritual masters have taught, one comes to know God rather by being grasped. It has been said that one starts by pursuing God like a hunter but when one's arrows have been exhausted, one must stop and either run away or wait to be pursued and captured in turn, with no idea of what the encounter will be like. This is the theme of Francis Thompson's famous poem with the strikingly irreverent title, "The Hound of Heaven". The concept of the God-centred or Spirit-filled human is even stranger country for the scientist, since anthropologists have no category into which they can classify this new kind of human, exemplified pre-eminently in Jesus but also by others in different religious traditions. What the seeker comes to experience is not God as a hypothetical almighty power in some distant heavenly realm but as something very real, present in some meaningful sense within us, linking and fusing our humanity directly to itself in a mysterious way. If there really is "that of God within all men", which was the conviction that brought Quakerism into existence, the scientific understanding of man, *Homo sapiens*, needs to be overhauled and a label invented to mark the existence of a significantly new type.

Biologically, modern humans are classified in the Linnaean convention of genus, species and subspecies as *Homo Sapiens Sapiens*. Technically a species is defined as an organism which can share its genes only with other members of the same species, that is to say, to interbreed with them. Blackberries are considered to be of the same species as raspberries, since they can be crossed to produce the stable hybrid loganberry, and greyhounds can similarly be crossed with many other types of dog to give lurchers. Several such self-enclosed species can be descended from the same genus and the genus is similarly a set of organisms which, although descended from a common evolutionary ancestor, the family, are unable to interbreed. Although this method of classification is far from watertight, humans, *Homo Sapiens Sapiens*, can be classified, and to that extent understood historically, as one among several subspecies of the species *Homo sapiens*, another being the familiar but long extinct *Homo Sapiens Neanderthalis*. From the fossil record palaeontologists have so far discovered fourteen other extinct subspecies, identified largely by brain size. There is, however, a great deal of guesswork and speculation involved, issuing in what have been called "taxonomic wars". It is, however, quality of consciousness, rather than cranial capacity which marks humans off from other apes and if Jesus were to be considered as a distinct human type or subclass, he would merit the classification of *Homo Sapiens Spiritualis*. So too anyone who had the same kind of consciousness, once its parameters were clearly defined. Such an assertion would be unacceptable to most anthropologists, but its logic is increasingly accepted by a more recent generation. Robin Dunbar, who is an evolutionary psychologist, can write in his authoritative *Human Evolution*, "The story of human evolution has conventionally always been told in terms of the bones and stones that make up the archaeological record - for the very good reason that this is often all we have to go on with any certainty and for the last half century archaeologists have been loath to stray far from the 'hard evidence' lest they be accused of being speculative. Yet the stones and bones skirt around what is perhaps the real story of evolution, namely the social and cognitive changes that, step by slow and uncertain step, gave rise to modern humans. it is here that the really big questions lie [2]." As will later be shown, Paul recognized Christians quite clearly as a new human type and, without any knowledge of biological science, the name he gave to it will prove to be remarkably appropriate when treating of modern spirituality.

The Pauline doctrine of God as Father, Son and Spirit marked a disconnect in Jewish theology. A similar word to Spirit, *ruach*, meaning "divine wind" can be found in the Jewish Bible, but is not emphasized, as this would have contradicted the monotheistic definition of God by which the Jews were self-defined. The Jewish religion itself arose from a theological disconnect, when, over a period of centuries, the Hebrews detached themselves from the polytheism which was the universal religion of their time and of all their neighbouring tribes. It is hard for us today to understand the importance of this breakout and how central to Judaism was its unalterable belief in a rigid monotheism. It is, of course, central also to Islam, and the call to prayer from minarets all over the world opens with, "God is great. There is one God and Mohamed is his prophet". The defining Jewish prayer, the Shema, was ,"Hear, O Israel, the Lord your God is one", and Jesus emphasized its importance to him by repeating this formula when he was asked what was the greatest commandment (Mark 12:29). The same words were uttered two thousand years later, prayed aloud by the Jews awaiting death in Nazi gas chambers as an expression of their Jewish identity which the Nazis were bent on eliminating from the world. The Shema was and remains the keystone of Judaic religion, and it is rarely noted that when Jesus claimed to be one with his "Father in heaven", he was laying a mine at the foundations of the religion he so passionately loved. That he almost certainly did not say it, is not strictly relevant, for by the time that the canon of authentic scriptures came to be compiled in the second century Paul's doctrine of the Holy Spirit had taken firm root, reinforced by the concept of the divine Logos taken from Greek philosophy. Would

Jesus have objected to his divinisation in this way? All the evidence suggests that he saw himself primarily as a radical reformer of Judaism, a healer and God's agent in ridding the Holy Land of Roman and Greek pagans. It is hard to imagine that he saw himself as the only son of God put on earth to be self-immolated for the sins of the world. That was Paul's invention and in this critical respect it is important in pursuit of truth to recognize that Paul, not Jesus, was the founder of Christianity.

With the decay of Christianity the term spirituality has undergone a fundamental shift of meaning, diluting its original sense and blurring the original meaning of spiritual as Spirit-filled and God-aware. A range of non-religious alternative spiritualities has been spawned in the past half century, some standing the original meaning on its head. Where once the concept of Christian spirituality exerted a unifying influence, we now have a bewildering and divisive array of different kinds of exclusive spiritualities - male and female, gay and straight, Eastern and Western, New Age and old-fashioned, to take only the most obvious. Among these the concept of a global spirituality can be found but usually devoid of details. The flow of books on all these spiritualities has become almost a flood. Interestingly, attempts have been made to do something practical about the decay of religious spirituality by inventing what might accurately be called non-religious religions. Karen Armstrong, a popular writer on a wide range of theological issues, initiated a *de facto* constitution for a world religion in 2008 in the *Charter for Compassion*. This was later elaborated in her 2011 book *Twelve Steps to a Compassionate Life*, the title clearly borrowed from the twelve steps of 'Alcoholics Anonymous'. Ewert Cousins, editor of the 107 volume work, *Classics of Western Spirituality,* also co-founded in 1998 *The World Commission on Global Consciousness and Spirituality*. Robert Muller, a long-serving Assistant Secretary-General of the United Nations campaigned tirelessly for that organisation to adopt an explicitly spiritual agenda, his best known book being entitled *New Genesis: Shaping a Global Spirituality*. These are by no means the only attempts to construct a global religion without actually using the term, but until the meaning of spirituality has been given focus and clarity it is hard to see how any of them will have much impact. The extent of this problem is surveyed in Professor Ursula King's 2009 book *The Search for Spirituality: Our Global Quest for Meaning and Fulfilment*. She herself does not offer a practical solution, other than suggesting that "it is perhaps more helpful to ask what spirituality does rather than what it is" and emphasizing, as do Armstrong, Cousins and others, that any new initiative must "express a new sense of the oneness of the world."

In all the variety of spiritualities (and King emphasizes that the plural form should be taken as a norm) there can be discerned common ideals which are often left undefined and taken for granted. "Spirituality" is used with implications of something higher than normally human, life-enhancing, ennobling, empathic, unselfish and fulfilling but not often is it associated with the sense of God-awareness that is associated with religious spirituality. Still less does it include the sense of oneness with God that is the distinguishing quality of Jesus and therefore, one must assume, of Christ-consciousness that the serious Christian is assumed to be seeking. It goes without saying that the new spirituality that is the concern of the present work will go along with developing compassion for our fellow humans and with nature, and with self-control, patience, generosity and other virtues, but the defining quality and *sine qua non* must be an habitual sense of oneness with our creating source and of identification with its will, and this takes spirituality into a strange and challenging place.

Spirituality and Mysticism

In the Christian tradition there seems to be an invisible barrier separating spirituality from mysticism. Once crossed, the spiritual seeker goes from a sense of oneness with Jesus, a companionship, to a sense of oneness with God. The former is largely a matter of solidarity and dedicated pursuit of the virtues that Jesus preached, the latter is an habitual sense of union with the Creating Power and a new sense of identity. Some may regard this as mystical and, as such, an anomaly in Christianity and in all religions, but the argument here is that it is a future new religious norm, the seeds of which can be seen in Paul's letters and the gospel of John. In an overview of what he called paradigms in Christianity, Hans Küng came to the conclusion that while Christianity displayed periodic mystical movements, it is not itself essentially a mystical religion, emphasizing (in bold type) that "Jesus himself was no mystic" and asserting that his reported saying, *I and the Father are one* "does not come from Jesus himself but from the Fourth Evangelist [3]." This is without doubt, for, as is generally recognized by scripture scholars, John's gospel at some point had a second introduction and other passages added by an unknown hand, clearly explaining the divinity of Jesus in the context of Greek philosophy. If it be accepted that mysticism is defined essentially as a sense of oneness with our creating source, Küng's categorical statement is self-contradictory, for whether or not these words were uttered, by Jesus, there surely can be no doubt that what set him apart was his habitual awareness of being "one with God", even though we may not fully understand the import of the phrase. It this sense of oneness essentially that set him apart from other humans and thus it should be the ultimate goal of Christianity and of every Christian but, unfortunately, is not. In direct opposition to Küng's understanding, if Jesus is regarded not as a divine quasi-human but as an evolutionary forerunner, it is perfectly natural to regard him as a mystic and to take the imitation of Christ in this respect as the defining core of Christianity. Perhaps one should talk of *Neo-Christianity* or perhaps a quite new term is now required, for this sense of oneness, which Küng regards as "at best an enrichment", becomes not only the essence of Christianity but a whole new way of life, calling for a life-changing decision. Küng's position is by no means unusual. Indeed, many authoritative theologians, including Adolf von Harnack, Karl Barth and Rudolf Bultmann strongly denied that mysticism of this unitary nature is integral to the Christian message which, they argued, essentially concerns salvation from sin through the atoning death of Jesus.

Others have been more sympathetic to the argument that the quest for oneness is at the heart of Christianity. Indeed, as this question is pursued, it appears that the difference in judgement is a clearly discernible fault line which has opened up and is putting Christianity in an existential crisis. In the Anglican tradition William Law (1686-1761) was more or less ostracised within his church for his advocacy of a mystical form of Christianity. In *The Spirit of Prayer* he could write, typically, "We are all of us by birth the offspring of God, more nearly related to Him than to each other," a phrase that could have been taken straight out of a Meister Eckhart sermon. Closer to our time, another Anglican, Evelyn Underhill, wrote at length about the mystical element of religion [4] and in her short work *Practical Mysticism*, subtitled "*A Little Book for Normal People*", argued strongly that it was a calling for all serious Christians, not just for a gifted few. While this extreme position is not common, it is shared by Eckhart and in agreement with Karl Rahner's thesis, to be treated in the following chapter, that Christianity must become a mystical religion or die.

What mysticism actually involves is answered by Underhill in Practical Mysticism thus:

> *Mysticism is the art of union with Reality. The mystic is a person who has attained that union ... in greater or less degree **or who aims at and believes in such attainment.** [5]*

The emphasis has been added to draw attention to the fact that while it customary to think of a mystic who has this new kind of consciousness fully developed, the reality is that even the greatest saints grow into it and the learner experiences it infrequently and weakly. Thus the word "mystic" is really quite inappropriate and a new (or almost new) term will be introduced later to cover all those who are on the path.

Underhill's definition is adequately precise and comprehensive in making four key points:

- At the heart of the mystical experience is a sense of oneness with a power or entity beyond ourselves which in itself is indescribable.
- Although the experience of oneness happens when normal faculties of knowing are switched off, it can vary in what might be called "depth" or "intensity".
- The "art" to which Underhill refers is a methodology which can reliably, but not automatically, lead to the "switching off" of normal consciousness, when a wordless and imageless kind of knowing takes over.
- The mystic is not necessarily one who has experienced this state in its most profound form but one who is convinced that a higher state of consciousness is possible and whose life is directed towards attaining it.

Perhaps one should add a fifth essential, too obvious to be noticed, that the process towards the state of oneness that is its end point cannot begin without a desire for it. This desire can initially be hardly more than a vague sense of dissatisfaction with life or of unfulfilled potential. Viewed thus, it can be seen that however feeble and confused it may be, the desire to know our ultimate source and, so to speak, have a relationship with it is a gift in the strongest sense of the word. It is what standard Christianity would call grace, but also a charism, that is, a gift given to the individual but for the benefit of the community. How it is to be transmitted is a question which opens up a new window in church organisation or what might be called *theologistics*, about which a few words will be said at the conclusion of this book. The main point here is that just as the human species began with apes who had a subconscious wish to try out walking on two legs, the next evolutionary development in man will come from those individuals who have a vague wish to know God and all that follows from it. It is foreseeable, though at the present seemingly fanciful, that the next branching in the Homo Phylum will occur as those humans who feel this need for God split off from those who have no such feeling and for whom belief in God is an obstacle to human progress.

Spirituality and Meditation

It is generally assumed that becoming spiritual calls for regular periods of meditation, virtually all guides advocating half an hour in the early morning and before retiring. Looking further into this prescription opens up fundamental questions of several kinds, a proper analysis of which would call for a whole new book. There is a genuine danger that if the wrong method is used, the end state will be not a deeper spirituality but a more entrenched self-centredness. All depends on whether the meditator is seeking to know the Source or seeking relief from various stresses. While there can be no objections raised against therapeutic meditation, it is necessarily a me-centred process and quite distinct from what might be called, to coin the phrase, "soul meditation". Yuval Noah Harari, whose books have been cited in the Introduction, writes about finding relief from a world made godless and meaningless by science (as he perceives it) by systematic meditation. His preferred and seeming effectively choice is the so-called 'Vipassana meditation', a Buddhist method in which all thoughts and imaginings are stilled and snuffed out by concentrating attention on one's breath, not on counting breaths, as in some other methods, but observing the act of breathing itself. In this context, as in Hindu theology, breath is taken to be either an analogue of life or life itself. From this perspective the meditator is in contact with a very this-worldly and commonsense source, with no risk of falling into religious superstition. Jarari himself engages for two hours each day in Vipassana meditation and spends two months each year on a meditative retreat, a luxury available to very few others.

Another and similar Buddhist method which has been popularised by Thich Nhat Hanh is "mindfulness meditation", in which attention is focused on what one is immediately engaged upon - preparing a meal, gardening, washing the car, changing the baby, etc., or just breathing, and all in a non-judgemental manner. Thich Nhat Hanh created a community, Plum Village, in France as a retreat centre for his teaching, which has achieved great popularity. There is no religious agenda: the benefits offered are essentially psychosomatic and include weight loss and relief from headaches. He does not claim to have invented this method and his basic ideas have been copied, or discovered independently, by other spiritual teachers and sometimes preached as "the power of now", the title of Eckhart Tolle's best-selling book. In most of these methods, belief in a divine power of some kind is no more than an option.

Several things are worth particular note in this brief account. The essential action in such meditation is a narrowing of the focus of one's normal consciousness to a point which is theoretically a timeless "now". This is superficially similar to what Jean-Pierre de Caussade called "the sacrament of the present moment" in his classic treatise *L'Abandon* [6], but there he teaches that acceptance of what God sends each moment is the most effective way to developing spirituality. Almost the identical doctrine was taught a thousand years earlier by the Sufi mystic Rabia of Basra (714-801), who is said to have reduced it simply to two words, "Don't complain". While there may be much more to be said than this, it can hardly be argued that one can achieve spirituality while indulging in constant complaint and criticism, and it is quite surprising how much of this we do every day, from slightly burnt toast for breakfast to inconvenient rain showers.

In general, methods of focused meditation are not usually linked to instruction in ascesis, such as Jesus gives in the gospel and Paul in his letters and which is to be found in Stoic literature. Ascesis here is used in the general sense of a discipline to be followed for self-development, rather than the more common usage, where an ascetic is someone who undergoes severe privation in order to achieve a spiritual goal or, in the case of Buddhism, a high degree of self-control. In the Christian tradition, where self-transformation is paramount, meditation and ascesis go together, and it is significant that when St Benedict set up his monasteries as "schools of the Lord's service" they were designed specifically as environments conducive to *conversio morum*, that is, change of behaviour. A lifelong attention to such change, in small and large things, must surely lead to a change of character, not greatly different from Pauline metanoia.

These few words must suffice to make the important point that spiritual meditation is different from what might be called secular or therapeutic meditation. While the latter may have beneficial effects on character, its prime purpose is, as the Buddha laid down, relief from suffering [7]. That is certainly a worthy aim in itself, especially when coupled with the prescribed requirement of compassion for our fellow man and all creatures, but it is not the same as spiritual meditation in the Christian tradition, the purpose of which is to "know God" as Jesus knew Him. The quotation marks are hardly needed to draw attention to the uncertainty of meaning in the phrase "knowing God". In this situation we may choose to conceive of "God", the inconceivable, either as a heavenly ruler, a loving father or as the primal source of all things, including, and especially, human consciousness. Consciousness is generated by a brain which is both transmitter and receiver and was not created out of nothing, as the Bible says, but from the Source itself. From this it follows that knowing God is a much more complex and richer thing than is commonly supposed, as will be illustrated in the following two chapters. It is a reflexive kind of thing, the Source knowing itself through my mediation. Or, looked at from God's side, the Source sees itself in me a holographic fragment. If that be true, then what it means to be human will need to be redefined.

Contemplation and Meditation

Not the least difficult in arriving at a workable system of meditation is that the word is commonly used more or less interchangeably with contemplation, both supposedly denoting the same thing, whereas they are, in fact, diametrically opposed in meaning. For most of the history of the Christian church, contemplation was held to be the mental activity that prepared one for a state of prayerfulness, meditation, when the mind was receptive rather than active. The standard material for contemplation was *lectio divina*, reading and reflecting on edifying books, especially the gospels. Meditation was ideally a period following this, when the lessons from the reading sank in. This sequence has been expressed simply as, "When I contemplate I think of God, but when I meditate, I just look at God and God looks at me." All this changed in the seventeenth century with the rise of so-called Ignatian spirituality, which added something new to the concept of prayer by blurring the difference between contemplation and meditation and promoting the active use of the imagination as a form of prayer, which was referred to, confusingly, as meditation. Imaginative meditation (in this new sense) is the basis of Ignatius of Loyola's *Spiritual Exercises*, which has had, and continues to have, great influence within, and even outside, the Catholic church. Imaginative prayer is at odds with what Teresa of Avila and others have called the prayer of quiet. What is at issue here is not a theological nicety but strikes at the very heart of what constitutes spirituality and, the present work will argue, at the future direction of human evolution. A brief account of the historical and theological background is necessary to explain why this is so. The following three passages will give a brief account of imaginative prayer. They are taken from a recent work by a Jesuit author, *What is Ignatian Spirituality?* [8].

> *Imaginative prayer is recognized as one of the hallmarks of Ignatian spirituality .... In his hands the imagination becomes a tool to help us know and love God. Ignatius presents two ways of imagining .... [In the first way] he asks us to "enter into the vision of God". God is looking down on our turbulent world. We see God intervening by sending*

> Jesus into the maelstrom of life. This type of imagining helps us to see things from God's perspective. The second method of imagining is to place ourselves within a story from the Gospels. We become onlookers .... We feel the hot Mediterranean sun beating down. We smell the dust, we feel the itchy clothing we're wearing, the sweat rolling down our brow .... Above all, we watch Jesus - the way he walks, his gestures, the look in his eyes, the expression on his face. We hear him speak the words that are recorded in the Gospel. We go on to imagine other words he might have spoken and other deeds he might have done.

The second quotation concerns the use of the imagination in inculcating moral and spiritual values.

> In this meditation Ignatius is using the imagery of standards - the battle flags that symbolize the identity of an army. One flag flies in front of the forces of Lucifer ... the other in front of the camp were Christ is leader. Ignatius would have us enter into this scene imaginatively, to see these two leaders in our mind's eye ... Lucifer on a throne, terrifying amidst smoke and fire and Christ standing on a lowly place, beautiful and attractive. What kind of instructions does Lucifer issue for waging the battle? How does Christ send forth his followers to win the hearts of others? We are to meditate upon the contrasting values.

The third quotation indicates the intended purpose of this kind of meditation:

> The practice of imaginative prayer teaches us who Jesus is and how he acts and how he decides. This kind of contemplation [note the switch from meditation] schools our hearts and guides us to the decisions that bring us closer to God

From these quotations it is clear that there is no room for the silent and wordless meditation that is typical of "the prayer of quiet", and that meditation in this very precise Ignatian sense is aimed at creating an idealised mental picture of the man Jesus, in order to know him better and imitate him. Insofar as spirituality hinges on "knowing God", rather than "knowing Jesus", which will be the theme of the following two chapters, there is clearly a disconnect and a critically grey area. To put it at its simplest, there is no obvious relationship with this kind of intellectually very active prayer and "the practice of the presence of God", which is the title of the short treatise of

Brother Lawrence (1614-1691), widely read and recommended, not least by John Wesley.

To examine the prayer of quiet or recollection, the counterpart of imaginative prayer, is to plunge into centuries of theological controversy and ecclesiastical politics, which suggests that something of great importance is at stake. One may date the beginning from the publication about the year 1300 of *The Mirror of Simple Souls* by Marguerite Porete, which treated spiritual development as increasing oneness with God. Although immensely popular at the time, it was unacceptable to the Church authorities, for a variety of reasons, but mainly because it encouraged the formation of spiritually oriented communities which were largely outside the official church structure. These "beguinages" thus constituted a threat not only to orthodox theology but to the political power of the Church. Although she was offered the chance to abjure her doctrine, Porete, who was no rebel, felt in conscience that she could not and was burned at the stake in Paris as a heretic. At about the same time, a similar doctrine of her teaching was being preached by Meister Eckhart (1260-1328) but based on an explicit new philosophy and indeed a new theory of God, which will be looked at more closely in Chapter 6. The 13th and 14th centuries in Western Europe were a flourishing period for mystical writing on the prayer of quiet and the anonymous *Cloud of Unknowing*, published about 1350 is one of several works which still speak with authority and which did not attract ecclesiastical censure. They suggest that mentally silent and wordless prayer had been practised before Eckhart, but he gave it new authority because of his position as a university teacher and high position in the Dominican order. In brief, Eckhart argued that we make contact with God in an essential way when the brain switches of all activity, for this is necessary in order for our soul, which contains a "spark" of shared divinity, to unite with its source. This brief explanation calls for clarification of the term "switching off", which will be provided later and is used here only to show that such prayer seems to run contrary to the commonsense understanding of mental prayer as the formulation in words of various emotional responses - asking, trusting, praising, submitting, etc. The very word "pray" is synonymous in English and other languages with asking or pleading. For Eckhart, only when we stop verbalising, memorising, anticipating and imagining, can we make direct contact with God at this deep psychological level and, no less important, can God make contact with us in a direct and wordless manner. It need hardly be said that Ignatian prayer, which is essentially the systematisation of common Christian belief, regards this approach as little more than idle reverie, perhaps even self-delusion. We instinctively think that in praying we must be doing something.

Eckhart's teaching, as is well known, was condemned by papal bull and his works were put on the Index of Forbidden Books in 1328. That seemed to put an end to controversy until about 1650, when the Spanish priest Miguel de Molinos published his *Spiritual Guide* (still in print) taking much the same approach to spirituality and the 'prayer of quiet' as Eckhart and Porete and greatly admired by eminent churchmen and lay persons alike. By this time the Society of Jesus, founded in 1541, had attained a position of moral and political authority within the Catholic Church, especially as it had been almost entirely responsible for stemming the tide of the Protestant Reformation. The Jesuit mixture of ideals, pragmatism and military discipline have a unique effect of raising the standards of spirituality, education and social awareness in the Catholic Church and attracted the best and most idealistic of young men, and later of women. The Jesuit constitution became a template for religious communities founded later, much as the American Constitution came to be used as a model for every subsequent new nation. The military ethos of discipline, unquestioning obedience, strategic and tactical planning which Ignatius deliberately built into the Jesuit Constitution has clear strengths, but its hidden weakness is that it is inherently resistant to radical change. This may be seen in the silencing of Pierre Teilhard de Chardin during his lifetime and, for a time, Karl Rahner. The latter is a more complex and interesting case, as will appear, for in later life he seems to have been trying to escape the limitations of imaginative prayer, as prescribed in the Spiritual Exercises, but caught in the dilemma that was posed by non-imaginative prayer.

Historically, one can see clearly the re-emergence of the doctrine of the 'prayer of quiet' in the doctrine of the Spanish priest, Miguel de Molinos (1628-1696) outlined in his *Spiritual Guide*. Its message is a variant of Eckhart's, essentially that a state of oneness with the divine can be achieved through the prayer of silence. At first, this was warmly received and commended by the then Pope's personal theologian and by many other churchmen and influential lay persons, but what was to follow was an exemplary case of religious totalitarianism at work. By the time that Molinos was writing and preaching this "new-but-old" doctrine of oneness the nascent Society of Jesus had grown so rapidly in numbers and in authority that it had effectively been put in charge of the Inquisition and had been described at the time as a church within the Church. The idea of a spirituality acquired through dreamy mental inactivity constituted a direct threat to both the principles and the power of the Society and steps were put in place to snuff it out. Among these were unattributed rumours that Molinos had engaged in sexual relations with some of the women to whom he was a spiritual director, although no evidence was ever found for this, and Molinos was of impeccable character. William James, no mean judge, describes him as "a spiritual genius, abominably condemned" in *The Varieties of Religious Experience*. Nevertheless, the smear has stuck and most scholars today tend to treat it, for lack of evidence, as a possibility, thus effectively demolishing the stature of Molinos as a spiritual guide. This was clearly the purpose of a dirty tricks department, which may or may not have originated with certain Jesuits in Rome. In any event, the end result was that Molinos was found guilty of heresy and condemned to life imprisonment.

His case was a *cause célèbre* and moved the Church to issue a papal ban in 1686 against this recurrent heresy under the blanket term of "Quietism". The method of prayer that goes by that name had never really gone away even after the censure of Porete and Eckhart and it is of interest that when Teresa of Avila wrote her *Way of Perfection*, about 1570, she removed a key chapter which was devoted to explaining and justifying the prayer of quiet [9]. The ban of 1698 effectively closed down any exploration into mystical religion within the Catholic Church for two centuries. Now it is a very live issue in Christianity more widely, but the deep rift between imaginative and wordless prayer remains and it would not be an exaggeration to say that the future of Christianity lies in its resolution. At issue is a stark new understanding of spirituality and two fundamental and related questions: is two-way communication with God really possible and does "knowing God" in its deepest sense entail not merely abandonment of the ego but its replacement by another kind of God-aware self. If the latter is true, authentic religion must eventually face a new definition.

Notes and References

1. David Tacey, *The Spirituality Revolution: The Emergence of Contemporary Spirituality*. London: Routledge, 2004. p.8.
2. Robin Dunbar, *Human Evolution*. London: Pelican, 2014. p. 3.
3. Hans Küng, *Christianity: Its Essence and its History*. London: SCM Press, 1995. p. 449.
4. See, e.g., her major work *Mysticism: The Nature and Development of Spiritual Consciousness*. Oxford:Oneworld Publications, 1993. First published in 1911 with several reprintings.

5. Evelyn Underhill, Practical Mysticism: *A Little Book for Normal People*. Guildford, Surrey: Eagle Publications, 1991 [1914], p. 2. In later years she drew back somewhat from her conviction that mysticism was for all, as the difficulties in attaining pure God-awareness, so to speak, became more apparent. Her doubts seem to have been raised by her later involvement with Eastern Orthodox theology and practice. From this experience she became aware that most people, and perhaps she herself, had a need not only for silent meditation but for the sensory experience of liturgy. This opens up very important questions, which it is not possible to address here.

6. Some controversy surrounds this work, usually translated as *Abandonment to Divine Providence*, which has given inspiration to many and has been translated into English in at least four editions in the last century. Caussade was a French Jesuit (1675-1751) of a rather stern disposition and the contrast in the style of his other works and this short treatise is the strongest evidence that it was not by his hand. Of particular present interest is the near certainty that the original author (who may have been a woman) borrowed Caussade's name and credentials in order to avoid being charged with Quietism, a point made by Dominique Salin in "The Treatise on Abandonment to Divine Providence," *The Way*, April 2007. pp.21-36. As will be treated in Chapter 6, the defined heresy of Quietism was a direct result of Meister Eckhart's radical new doctrine of spirituality.

7. Escape from suffering must be understood within the framework of death and rebirth of successive reincarnations, each providing an opportunity to become more virtuous until one passes the threshold of purification into nirvana, when the cycle ends.

8. David L. Fleming, SJ, *What is Ignatian Spirituality?* Chicago:Loyola Press, 2008. pp. 72, 94.

9. This is Chapter 31, which was restored by Alison Peers in his definitive English translation (NY:Dover Publications, 2012. pp. 200-210). It contains statements such as the following. "I want to describe this Prayer of Quiet ... as the Lord has been pleased to teach it to me, perhaps in order that I might describe it to you .... This is a supernatural state [in which] all the faculties are stilled, the soul realises that it is now very close to God and that, if it were but a little closer, it would become one with Him through union." (p. 210) It is probable that she removed this chapter on the advice of her spiritual director, who was more aware than she of the risk of official censure that it would cause.

CHAPTER 5
THE RAHNER PARADOX

The devout Christian of the future will be either a 'mystic', one who has experienced something, or he will not be anything at all.

Karl Rahner [1]

The need to know God

Karl Rahner (1904-1984) is generally acknowledged as one of the most influential Christian theologians of the twentieth century and is certainly one of the most thought-provoking. His output was immense, covering almost every theological field, from systematic to pastoral. He was not a popular theologian, in the sense of being widely read by non-scholars, for the complexity of his thought was matched by the impenetrability of his prose. Indeed, his brother and fellow Jesuit Hugo once said that to understand him he often found it easier to go to translations from the original German, where the translator had already done the heavy lifting in clarifying Karl's densely interwoven thought.

Rahner's theology was at once conservative and radical. While he was critical of the Roman Catholic Church, and of Christianity more generally, he was unable to think objectively about either, having been brought up within the boundaries of the mythology. He could see many of the Church's shortcomings, but could never fully stand outside the institution which both propagated the myth and was created by it. He was formed and lived within a framework of assumptions to which he was inevitably blind and hence unquestioning. This is not stated as a personal criticism, for we are all trapped within a cultural matrix with aspects that are as invisible to us as the back of our head but which are perfectly clear to anyone from a different culture. In one important sense, which the present book explores, anyone who can rescue us from this group blindness is a saviour. Rahner was not trained in any of the sciences and his philosophical framework was inherited from Heidegger, who was outstandingly a word analyst, and from neo-Thomist thinkers, particularly from Joseph Maréchal, his fellow Jesuit and teacher at university [2]. Maréchal was a prominent exponent of the thought of Thomas Aquinas, whose system was based on Aristotelian proto-science. Rahner's thought processes were therefore essentially pre-Newtonian, pre-evolutionary and, in a word, pre-scientific.

Despite this conservatism, Rahner's ideas were at one time considered so close to heretical that the authorities in Rome forbade him to publish. Yet within months of the ban he was appointed as the chief *peritus*, or expert, at the Second Vatican Council (1962-65) and was thereafter rehabilitated. Obviously the same authorities in the church's opaque bureaucracy which had condemned him had come to the pragmatic conclusion that some fresh thinking was needed to counter the visible decay of Catholicism in the West and saw Rahner as the best chance of providing what was required – in a nutshell, reform without revolution, change without change! Herein lies Rahner's special importance in the wider theme of spiritual evolution.

He is probably best known for two controversial proposals, namely the existence of what he called "anonymous Christians" and the requirement, as quoted at the head of this chapter, for the serious Christian to be a "mystic", Rahner himself enquoting the word to indicate that its meaning is in question. He then specifies that by "mystic" he is referring not to someone who has visions and ecstasies or hears voices but who has

> *a genuine experience of God emerging from the very heart of our existence*

It follows then that both concepts, i.e., the anonymous and mystical Christian, are in opposition to a religion which bases membership not on the quest for a relationship with God but on acceptance of a particular belief system and which is focused on worshipping an external divinity, rather than seeking a deepening communication with it. The concept of anonymous Christianity implies that humans can become Christlike – i.e., fully developed spiritually – without need for a church or for the whole theological and administrative apparatus we call "The Church". Indeed, the term "anonymous Christian" implies that one could become in some essential sense a Christian without ever having heard of Jesus or read the gospels; but in what this essential Christianity consists is never spelled out. Significantly, the dissolution of religious boundaries which is suggested by "anonymous Christianity" can also be found in Dietrich Bonhoeffer's equally well known phrase, "religionless Christianity". Both raise the crucial questions, why bother to become a Christian, what unique benefits are offered to the spiritual seeker by the Christian community? An equally interesting question arising is what could possibly be meant by the terms "anonymous Moslem" or "anonymous Buddhist".

The implication that Christianity of the future would be a mystical religion invites controversy, for if Rahner's assertion is accepted, the Christian churches, which do not offer or encourage mystical experience, would surely find themselves in opposition to this new form of Christianity, as indeed they have been in the past. This comment opens up painful and wide-ranging historical issues which must be bypassed here with reference only to individuals like Miguel de Molinos, Jeanne Guyon and Meister Eckhart who were forbidden by the Catholic Church to teach and to Marguerite de Porete and the Quaker Mary Dyer, who were executed, the former in France and the latter in Massachusetts, "hanged like a flag for others to take example by." All were effectively outlawed for teaching the kind of experiential Christianity which Rahner considers an essential component of future Christianity. All these apparent innovations were lumped together as "Quietism", which was classified as a heresy and formally condemned by the papacy in 1687, a ban which has never been repealed. Sufism, an almost identical mystical movement in Islam, originating around the ninth century was persecuted even more violently and continues to be persecuted, with hundreds of deaths in Pakistan reported since the year 2000. Clearly those rare souls who sought the oneness which Jesus experienced and manifested are more often than not, regarded as unexplainable exceptions, rarely as examples to be imitated. Often their higher than human status is acknowledged after death. Quite typically, after Teresa of Avila died, parts of her body were cut off to be venerated as holy relics. Her left hand was later seized by General Franco and became his personal possession, which he kept by his bedside until his death. Thus spirituality without intellectual foundation easily degrades into jujuism.

References to the Christian as mystic are scattered throughout Rahner's voluminous writing and when analysed in context, their revolutionary force is somewhat diminished. In one major work he defines mysticism, for instance, in the following contradictory and rather evasive way:

> *We do after all possess a vague empirical concept of Christian mysticism; the religious experiences of the saints, all that they experienced of closeness to God, of higher impulses, of visions, inspiration, of the consciousness of being under the special and personal guidance of the Holy Spirit, of ecstasies, etc., all this is comprised in our understanding of the word mysticism,* **without our having to stop here to ask what exactly it is that is of ultimate importance in all this, and in what more precisely this proper element consists.** [3]

The emphasis has been added because that is precisely the question that surely *must* be asked if mysticism, still awaiting clear definition, is to be adopted as a new norm, rather than assumed to be the exceptional experience of a few recognized saints. This and similar definitions in other places lead to two obvious conclusions: firstly, that there is nothing distinctively Christian in mysticism of this general kind. With some reservations Rahner's list would be perfectly acceptable to, say, the Sufi mystic Rumi and the great Hindu teacher Shankara. Secondly, the list omits what Jesus himself seems to have regarded as the core of his own form of mystical awareness, namely, directing his life to doing the assumed will of an assumed creator. It drove him like a hunger: in the words of John's gospel, "Doing the will of Him who sent me is my food" (4:34). This fusing of self-will and divine will can hardly be taken as just an exotic footnote to orthodoxy, for it is the very factor that made Jesus stand out from ordinary humans. From this perspective the quest for a union of wills that so defines Jesus should surely be the very definition of Christian orthodoxy.

Rahner refers to his revolutionary doctrine as "everyday mysticism", thus assuming that it is, or should be, a norm rather than the exception. As a doctrine, however, it must be brought together from several books and smaller pieces in his corpus [4]. Because of his unquestioned commitment to the Catholic Church and to the Society of Jesus, it is always couched with some ambiguity and continually skips around the question, is this mainstream Christianity or an optional add-on or a necessary innovation? Certainly it is far from credal. What he is offering and seeking for himself he describes variously as "an encounter with God ... God's self-communication ... the Silent infinite ... Your very self in the depths of my heart", but perhaps the most telling attempt to communicate what he has experienced and hopes to experience more deeply is to be found in his desire to meet the divine reality directly, unmediated by words or symbols. His desire is for:

> *You Yourself, not just a concept of You, not just the name which we ourselves have given you.*

That is the nub of his doctrine and it is worth noting that it is both very Eckhartian and very Quaker in spirit. Eckhart talks of this union as "ground to Ground" on the assumption that humans share the essence of the divine creator. Quakerism is, of course, distinguished by belief in "that of God within all men" and the centrality of the silent meeting, when normal consciousness regularly dissolves in the "gathered" or "centred" meeting. The experience is impossible to convey in words, but in the roughest possible way it may be described as a sense of profound calm and of being taken over by a higher kind of consciousness. The individual and the group on such occasions experience a state which fully justifies the term transcendent, but it must be emphasized that this experience comes when it comes and the few words above in description are purely indicative and in no way inclusive of what actually happens. There seems to be a kind of entrainment which reaches down to a deeper level of consciousness, where oneness is felt. Against this minimal background perhaps it could be said that much of what Rahner sought was there in plain sight before him. It should be noted, however, that Quakers, in Britain at least, report unofficially that the experience of the gathered meeting, which was once a normal and expected occurrence, is becoming quite rare. This is to be expected in the present secular and self-centred age, as belief in the biblical God ebbs away and is not replaced by a coherent theory of the creating power. Quakerism, which is in principle "open to new light from whatever source", has opened itself to the soft agnosticism which has become a kind of unofficial religion for many non-religious individuals today. The phenomenon of the gathered meeting seems clearly to be, at one level, a psychological entrainment effect. Thus if most of those present have no strong sense of the reality of God, it is unlikely that sitting in silence will produce in the group as a whole the well attested sense of presence, which is what Rahner appears to be seeking.

The religious conclusions that flow from Rahner's *cri de coeur* – for it is nothing less – are disconcerting and merit a book-length analysis. He appears to be pointing to a radical deficiency in the religion that he had spent his life serving. Christianity has come to be regarded as the belief system rather than the Christ-experience. More bluntly, the churches have kept the doctrinal peel and thrown away the experiential fruit, which is what Rahner seems to be saying. The myth has become the message. For if Paul's Christianity is defined as acquiring "the mind of Christ" and if John's gospel gives us an accurate representation of Christ's habitual consciousness, then this hunger for the unmediated experience of God should surely be the calling of all Christians. Perhaps it would be better not to call it mystical, for the word has several inappropriate connotations.

Rahner does not refer back to Paul's central teaching about seeking the mind of Christ but, rather, emphasizes that,

> *The modern spirituality of the Christian involves courage for solitary decision contrary to public opinion, the lonely courage analogous to that of the martyrs of the first century of Christianity.* [5]

That is a jaw-dropping statement, implying that the officially recognized churches today stand as obstacles to truth and spiritual progress, as once did the pagan cults of the Roman Empire. That spiritual seekers can expect to be martyred by the churches that they love and from which they take their identity is food for thought indeed.

Light from the East?

That something essential is missing or has been lost in Christianity is evidenced by the number of Christian writers, and Catholics in particular, who have gone to Hinduism and Buddhism in the belief that they would find it there. From the mid-twentieth century there has been a steady stream of theologians and philosophers seeking enlightenment through either mind altering drugs or meditational disciplines and sometimes, like Aldous Huxley and Alan Watts, through both. A large number of seekers, most famously the Beatles, have gone to India, found a guru and lived for shorter or longer periods in ashrams or to Japan, where they have put themselves under the discipline of a Zen master. Many questions arise from considering this phenomenon but, centrally, "what are they seeking that cannot be obtained in the West and have they found it? Is Western religion unable in principle to provide it?" As with Rahner, there appears to be a personal need to experience a Higher Power directly and usually a de-emphasis of the fact that orthodox Buddhism does not accept the existence of a creating power, and certainly not one which intervenes in human affairs [6]. The aim of Buddhism is to escape from suffering and through control of the mind and virtuous behaviour escape from the cycle of birth, death and rebirth to achieve the perfect, timeless bliss of nirvana. Is the Buddhist meditator experiencing God unintentionally or without awareness of it? Many would sidestep the question by saying that Buddhists believe in a higher power, but as a principle, rather than as a heavenly person, but the fact remains that Christianity is centred on belief that God is a loving entity and is in touch with humans in a humanlike way and we with Him, and this has no place in orthodox Buddhism.

 The best known of the religious writers who went east is probably the Trappist monk Thomas Merton (1915-1968), who travelled extensively in the cause of dialogue with Buddhist monks and in search of common ground between them and Christian monks. The Benedictine Bede Griffiths (1906-1993) spent much of his adult life in India attempting to find a creative combination of monastery and ashram, but in the end had to settle for little more than hopes of a deeper ecumenism between the two religions. This is broadly true also of the Sri Lankan Jesuit Aloysius Pieris (b.1934) and the Spanish-Indian Raimon Panikkar (1918-2010). The Jesuit William Johnston (1925-2010) spent many years in Japan and wrote extensively about his experiences. In his autobiography he says, "I must turn my eyes towards Asia, where I see the rise of a new mystical Christianity that, in dialogue with Asian spirituality, will wonderfully serve the world" [7]. It is probably fair to say, however, that overall his conclusions lead towards the impossibility of productive dialogue. Most controversially, he seems to see what might be called the mystical experience of non-dualism or selflessness as a natural extension of Christian theology and practice, noting that "many theologians hold that Christian mysticism is no more than an intensification of the ordinary Christian life ... a deepening of that faith and love that every true Christian possesses", so that "every convinced Christian is a mystic in embryo" [8]. That conclusion is controversial and critical and at odds with the argument of the present work, which is that the transition to mystical awareness is both a religious and evolutionary step-change and normally calls for a specific decision. No theistic religion segues naturally into mysticism, defined simply as a reunion of oneness, and thence to the habitual experience of oneness, for by definition theism is about a creating god which is separate from what it has created. It would be more accurate to see theisms not as different routes to the same mystical destination but as train journeys towards a common junction, where all must alight and board the same train to a common destination, previously unsuspected.

Perhaps the most significant of these cross-cultural explorers was Henri Le Saux (1910-1973), a French Benedictine, who went all the way into Hinduism, undergoing extensive training from a guru before becoming one himself and recognized as a swami, taking on the name Abhishiktananda. His writings, mostly in French, circle round the extreme dissonance which he experienced between the Christian and Hindu narratives. At first he was inclined to think that all religions find their fulfilment in Christianity but as the years passed he became more inclined to think that this was more true of Vedantic (i.e., advaitic) Hinduism, simply because the experience of non-duality which he sought was there quite explicitly, but hard to find in orthodox Christianity. Against this, however, it was the Christian narrative that made sense to him as a "theory of reality": he had, in his words, "a visceral attachment to the Christian myth" [9]. In the end he came to see that liturgical prayer which had been at the centre of his life as a Benedictine monk as "a game that has to be left behind" and was faced with a seemingly irreconcilable dilemma, for the Catholic Church treats it as "an absolute in itself", whereas it is an obstacle to the experience of oneness, which he had come to see clearly as the *raison d'être* of religion. Elsewhere he says, "All was agony at my Mass .... I need to be freed from the Mass." Strangely, he did not see Hindu liturgy as an obstacle in the same way, seemingly because advaita, the quest for oneness with the divine, was the central goal for vedantic Hinduism, but not so for orthodox Christianity. His thoughts on this are worth quoting at some length:

> *Advaita is so overpowering - disappearance in the One! And so is Hindu worship, at least in its purest manifestation - the offering of flowers and milk to the bare stone - phallic-shaped, but nothing obscene in the idea - placed in the holy of holies, the cave, that small dark chamber deep in the heart of the temple, which one only reached after passing through numerous courtyards and halls .... I am torn, rent in two, between Christ and my brothers .... When I pray per Christum, they [sc. Hindu worshippers] cannot follow me. And I can no longer rejoice in our feasts as formerly and I cannot unite myself to my people in their symbolic religion, **because I am a priest of the true religion**, and thus I fail to have communion with my people in what is the highest and most divine in them.* [10]

The emphasis has been added to bring home the point that, like Karl Rahner, he feels trapped between his belief that the Christian narrative is a uniquely true theory of reality, a creation story in the widest frame, and his deepest feeling that it is cutting him off from the direct experience of God, which he has found in Hinduism. Almost as in a mirror image, Le Saux (to use the name that he deliberately gave up) sees Hindu liturgy and its plethora of half-human gods and fantastic stories of their behaviour as acceptable because advaitism is the essential core of Hinduism. The problem now taking shape is this: is it possible to have a religion which goes straight for the experience of oneness with God and has a believable narrative and a developmental praxis, including liturgy, at the same time. The whole thrust of the present work is to provide evidence that it is not only possible but that if the challenge is rejected, existing religions of all stripes will become stagnant pools in the historical flow which has taken us from ape to human and now offers to take us to the transhuman, the Christlike, and beyond even that.

The essence of Christianity

The more one reflects on the implications of identifying Christ-consciousness with a sense of oneness with the divine reality, the more its revolutionary nature comes into focus, and one sees with increasingly clarity the astonishing way in which Paul came to recognize Jesus of Nazareth as the kernel of a new kind of religion. The quest for oneness certainly stands out starkly against the less demanding kind of religion that passes for Christianity today, and equally against other belief systems. Stoicism, Confucianism and Buddhism are all noble ways of life, but none is concerned with developing a divine-human relationship of the intimate kind that Jesus manifested. One can certainly find in Stoic literature references to a divinity, often to divinities in the plural, which are taken to be real but rather distant and Epictetus stands out in teaching conformity with the divine will as a primary virtue. In general, the emphasis in Stoicism is on developing human virtues, generosity, patience, compassion, etc., and particularly self-discipline and emotional control on the way to becoming an ideal human. In this it differs little from Buddhism except that the aim of Buddhism is to do away with suffering by escaping from illusion and the Buddha taught that the last illusion that must be abandoned is the concept of a creating god that intervenes in life's affairs. There is no room in Buddhism for the concept of a loving God, which is, of course, central in the teaching of Jesus. How then shall we judge the rightness of *a reasoned belief* in the reality of a divine power with which communication is possible and how shall we justify the *feeling* that such communication is the meaning and purpose of life? Some individuals know and feel the immediacy of the divine intuitively, as did Jesus, some are open to being convinced, but many admirable individuals have no sense of this at all and would agree with Freud that to talk about the God-human relationship as the meaning of life is an infantile delusion, blocking human progress.

Doing the will of God is a phrase worn smooth of meaning by familiarity in religious circles and yet it is a most radical statement in the context of human evolution. It raises the question: is conscious and deliberate unification with the will of a higher power an optional add-on to the broad ideal of human development, or is it the core? Is this union of wills implicitly the definition of a higher kind of human which will either follow on or co-exist with *Homo Sapiens*? Are we supposed to take seriously a proposal that Christians, as imitators of Jesus, should be defined not by adherence to a creed but by habitual awareness that they are attempting to carry out the *hypothesized purpose of a hypothesized reality to which we give the identifying label*

"God"? How many of the hundreds of millions who would describe themselves as Christians feel that their life is given meaning and purpose by commitment to this principle? How many would resign on the spot from the Church if such a commitment was made an explicit condition of membership? What actually does the phrase "doing God's will" mean? How does it differ from the Islamic principle of the will of Allah? Is it at base an excuse for fatalism? Or, to come at the question from another angle, does that vague word "spirituality" have any meaning if it is not centred on accepting this commitment, not just as an abstract ideal but as a conviction, even a gut feeling, and a way of life? Abbot John Chapman says in his *Spiritual Letters* that if someone were to ask the genuine Christian what he or she is doing, their automatic response should be something like, "in general, doing the will of God; at this particular moment washing the dishes, walking the dog, watching the television, etc." The more one thinks about the idea of devoting one's life to "doing the will of God" the more disturbing and thought-provoking it becomes.

From a secular point of view, a way of life based on the assumed intentions of an unknown creating power is not merely infantile but dangerous, for history shows innumerable instances of the most inhuman actions that have been justified as "doing the will of God". Examples are hardly necessary, from the atrocities of the so-called Islamic state seen on our television screens, to the genocide by the Jews of the original inhabitants of Canaan on the instruction of their god. Psychiatry recognizes "doing God's will", often accompanied by hearing his voice, as one of the most common forms of paranoid schizophrenia. Is it reasonable then to even consider that in this particular regard we are seeing in Jesus the emergence of a new type of human of which he is a template and blueprint? Is it possible that he and other outstanding mystics, by no means all Christians, who preach this doctrine, are as distinct from and superior to the average decent human as the normal human today is superior to his illiterate Stone Age forbears? We find ourselves here at a crossroads of decision which is rarely, if ever, explicitly required by conventional religion. Do we want to remain human or press on towards the trans-human as exemplified in Jesus? The more one thinks about it, the more unreasonable it appears that each of us, classified zoologically as members of Hominidae, the family of the great apes, can be on speaking terms with the unknown power that brought billions of galaxies into existence. It may be that we are in touch not with this ultimate power which is the source of everything but with some lesser aspect of it, a subordinate "manager god" such as the Demiurge that Plato conjectured, or with the Holy Spirit that Jesus offered to send (John

14:26). However, it does not seem as it would make any practical difference in the quest to arrange one's life in order to do God's will. The main thing is, as Eckhart emphasized, is that God in the most unqualified sense must be the ultimate source of our consciousness. We know now through cosmological science that there is a historical link between us and the God who brought the cosmos into being and that realisation is the starting point of a religious revolution.

Notes and References

1. Karl Rahner, "Christian Living Formerly and Today" in *Theological Investigations* VII, trans. David Bourke. NY: Herder and Herder, 1971. p. 15.
2. It is very possible that the seeds of Rahner's 'late-life need' to know God directly may lie in Maréchal's earlier influence, particularly through his *Studies in the Psychology of the Mystics*.
3. "The Ignatian Mysticism of Joy in the World," in *Theological Investigations* III. London: Darton, Longman and Todd, 1963. pp. 277-293.
4. English translations of his main thoughts can be found in The *Mystical Way in Everyday Life: Sermons, Prayers and Essays* (NY: Orbis books), *Encounters with Silence* (South Bend, IN: St Augustine's Presss) and *Prayers for a Lifetime* (NY: Crossroad Publishing). *Theological Investigations* is a weighty compendium of most of a lifetime's thinking, both systematic and occasional.
5. Karl Rahner (eds. Karl Lehmann and Albert Raffelt), *The Practice of Faith: a Hand book of Contemporary Spirituality*. NY: Crossroad Publishing, 1986. p. 21.
6. The *Wikipedia* entry for "Creator in Buddhism" states categorically, "Buddhist thought consistently rejects the notion of a creator deity."
7. William Johnston, *Mystical Journey: An Autobiography*. NY: Orbis Books, 2006, p. 1. See also *Christian Zen: A Way of Meditation*. Fordham UP, 1997.
8. William Johnston, *The Still Point: Reflections on Zen and Christian Mysticism*. Fordham UP, 1989. pp. 26-27.
9. The quotation is taken from Shirley du Boulay's biography, *The Cave of the Heart*. NY: Orbis, 2005, p. 98.
10. Op cit. p. 97.

CHAPTER 6
ECKHARTIAN REVOLUTION

Man's curiosity searches past and future and clings to that dimension. But to apprehend the point of intersection of the timeless with time, is an occupation of the saint.

T.S.Eliot [1]

Eckhart's vision of God

Meister Eckhart (1260-1328) shares many traits with other spiritual writers but stands out in three particular ways, namely, in putting forward a new theory and model of God, in attempting to communicate his spiritual experience within the scientific framework of his time and in teaching that the mystical life is not exceptional but the potential calling of the average human being. This claim is not common among spiritual writers and its validity depends very much on how mysticism is defined. If Eckhart is right in believing that ordinary men and women, following the right procedures, can achieve an habitual sense of oneness with God, he can be seen as the precursor of a paradigm change not only in Christianity but in religion itself.

In contrast to the strict Jewish monotheism of Jesus and the trinitarian God of Paul, Eckhart preached a dualistic understanding of God, using the German words *Gott* and *Gottheit* to mark the distinction. In his writings he switches constantly between the Dualistic and the Trinitarian models, which is to be expected, since, however revolutionary his vision, he was constrained by the theological paradigm within which he had grown up and had to use its categories to communicate with his readers or, more accurately, his audience, since his message was given mostly in sermons. The conflict between orthodox trinitarianism and his novel dualism is rarely noted by commentators, as he maps conventional theology onto his new doctrine, using ambiguous expressions such as the "birth of Christ in the soul" when he should more accurately be talking of the onset of the *Gottheit*. The distinction between *Gott* and *Gottheit* is usually translated into English as between *God* and *The Godhead*, or *God* and *The Deity*, but *Gottheit* is an unusual word, almost impossible to translate into English and probably most other languages. "Godness" or "Godship" or "Goddity" would probably be somewhat closer than "Godhead", since the suffix *–heit* in German, as in nouns like *Freiheit* (freedom) or *Schönheit* (beauty), expresses a state or quality, rather than a thing or a person. *Gottheit* refers to the total timeless reality of the Primal Source, what philosophers would call the unknowable *Ding an sich*, the thing in itself, whereas *Gott* signifies our limited human perception of it. In this Eckhart anticipates by five centuries the influential theory of knowledge of Emmanuel Kant [2].

The significance of this is that by using the word "God" in normal speech we force the Ultimate Reality into our restricted understanding as humans. Eckhart's controversial point is that we humans share the timelessness of the Godhead, even though it is impossible for us to imagine in any way, let alone put our knowledge into words, the ultimate reality, the *ens realissimum* which exists outside the boundaries of time and space. It did not create everything in the normal sense, as a builder creates from an existing material, or even from nothing, as Judaeo-Christianity teaches, for in this timelessness there was only God, not even a nothing. Where God came from is a question that can have no possible answer, and thinking about it only brings on mental vertigo, but the fact that we and the universe are here is proof that there is an ultimate timeless cause of some kind beyond our limited understanding. This timeless "something" is the *Gottheit* and Eckhart's perfectly logical case is that everything in our three-dimensioned universe must have emerged from the *Gottheit* itself, and that is particularly and dramatically true of human consciousness. We are made from the divine being, its very essence, in a special way, for by virtue of our consciousness we can re-imagine, reflect and, in some sense, reactivate this timeless reality. It seems at first like Alice-in-Wonderland theology: the infinite God creates us from its own substance and, in return, we enable it to manifest in our time-bound mini-universe, granted that this mini-universe is billions of light years in extent. From this perspective prayer is nothing more than an ongoing act of consent for this reactivation to happen. What we tend to think of as "knowing God" is in reality a handing over of our sovereign self and its replacement with a divine self and will. It might be seen, rather crudely, as a transfusion of Spirit or divine consciousness. Perhaps the easiest way to get a feeling for Eckhart's message is to emphasize that this transformation is the outcome of a two-way communication that takes place without words. He sometimes refers to the Godhead as "a desert of silence."

In proposing that we should seek communication with God in silent, wordless meditation Eckhart emphasizes that we partake of the timelessness of the Godhead. In his words,

> *In the stillness there exists only the present instant .... A Now which always and without end is itself new .... There is no yesterday nor any tomorrow, but only Now, as it was a thousand years ago and as it will be a thousand years hence.* [3]

and

> *There is nothing in creation so like God as silence.*

These are deep philosophical waters, but from Eckhart's doctrine it follows that religion clearly acquires a new purpose, namely, to activate a latent sense of oneness with our ultimate source, to think God's thoughts after Him. Growth into this new state comes in the accepted way through verbalised prayer in the normal way, edifying reading and reflection (*lectio divina*) and radical modification of behaviour but, critically, silent prayer is the key method where "deep calls to deep". Wordless communication of this intimate kind may begin with a verbalising of thought and emotion but its aim is to cross over into mental silence, when the normal activity of the brain ceases. What happens then is the kind of direct, unmediated experience of God (Eckhart's *Gottheit*) that Rahner sought. Do we connect with God in the silence or would it be truer to say that (in a limited human context) the silence itself is God? Certainly, it is felt as a fullness rather than an emptiness and of being in some way in touch with a higher power. While this is two-way communication, our part is not to speak back but simply look, although that is not a fully appropriate metaphor. This is in direct contrast with the view that the most beneficial kind of prayer comes with great mental activity - asking, praising, confessing, promising, imagining and, in general, talking to God. The state of silent worship is often described as an "active passivity", an expression which indicates that during this experience all normal brain activity ceases. In the words of a modern spiritual teacher,

> *What keeps us from knowing God is the unceasing activity of the human mind. When we learn to be still, the mind of God can function in us. Or, to put the same truth in another way, when the surface levels of the mind become stilled, the inner levels can work in unison with the divine mind.* [4]

From a Hindu and theosophical viewpoint, Krishnamurti enlarges on this using a different metaphor:

> *Silence which is not just the ending of noise is only a small beginning. It is like going through a small hole to an*

> *enormous, wide expansive ocean, to an immeasurable timeless state. But that state one cannot understand verbally. [5]*

Eckhart insists that the ability to find the silence is at the heart of "having the mind that was in Christ", which Paul preached as the purpose of Christianity. What is revelatory in Eckhart's teaching (or heretical, depending on one's standpoint) is that all humans, by virtue of being human, have the potential to share the same awareness of being one with God that is conventionally taken to be a unique attribute of Jesus and is of the essence of mysticism. It need hardly be said, though, that there are different degrees of potential and different levels of experiencing the silence, when all mental chatter ceases and self-awareness fades into the background and then goes out like a light switched off.

The religious significance of this divine-human oneness is at the centre of Eckhart's teaching and is continually emphasized. In his words,

> *There has never been such an absolute union, for the union of the soul with God is far closer than that of the body with the soul.*

And in an attempt to shock his hearers into understanding, or at least provoke them into serious thinking about God, he says in one place,

> *Where I am there is God.*

Oneness: Orthodoxy or Heresy

This shocking assertion is simply a statement of the obvious in Eckhart's theological and scientific thought-frame. Whether or not it would be so in the thought world of Jesus is an interesting question, for, as a Jew, he would have been brought up in the orthodox belief that God was one and undivided. The immediate reaction of most good Christians today is likely to be that Eckhart's statement is nonsense and dangerous nonsense at that. The man in the street would probably say he was deranged, like the poor chap who thinks he is Napoleon. It is surely significant that in Mark's gospel Jesus is so far considered out of his mind that his family felt they had to put him under restraint [6]. So the question arises, was Eckhart a prophet ahead of his time (as prophets are by definition) or was he a danger not only to religion but to commonsense and sanity? First it must be said that the quest for oneness which Eckhart makes so defining an element of Christianity is not unique, but seems to hover half-expressed in many other spiritual writers. In Julian of Norwich (1342-1416) we find it very explicitly:

> *It is a great understanding to see and know inwardly that God who is our creator dwells in our soul, and it is a far greater understanding to see and know inwardly that our soul which is created dwells in God in substance, of which substance, through God, we are what we are.* ***And I saw no difference between God and our substance, but, as it were, all God; and still my understanding accepted that our substance is in God.*** (Emphasis added). [7]

On first encounter, such statements as the above cannot but sound like heresy, asserting, as they do, an unwarranted and improper claim of intimacy with God which is not to be found in the gospels or the creed. The proper relationship to God which Jesus clearly taught is between father and child, embodied in the Lord's Prayer which is addressed "Our Father who art in heaven". This familiarity, it should be said, was a revolutionary extension of Jewish theology, which is founded on, and still retains, a primitive understanding of a distant deity, basically a heavenly potentate, which may be loving but is ruthless when disobeyed, as befits an all-powerful ruler and creator. The concept of a God who loves one so personally as Jesus preached would have been at the least unorthodox to his hearers and without doubt would have sounded at least somewhat irreverent. Jews were brought up to believe in a loving God, but one who loved their tribe and had singled it out. The sense of a deeply personal relationship with God does appear in the writings of some of the prophets, notably Job and Jonas, but almost in the form of complaint and argument with God. It appears elsewhere in the vast corpus of Jewish theological and poetic literature, notably perhaps in Martin Buber's influential *Thou and I* [8], but Eckhart goes beyond it and seems to take impossible liberties in trying to convince his hearers that God is always on our side. In one sermon, considering his own insignificance, he says that God loves him to the point of foolishness, and in another goes so far as to say that "God winks at the sinner." The Old Testament God, "the God of Abraham, Isaac and Jacob," would certainly not wink at the sinner, nor indeed would the God of Jesus, loving and forgiving as He is presented in the beautiful story of the Prodigal Son. Eckhart is struggling to take us with him into a deeper understanding of the divine-human and human-divine relationship.

This God who colludes in our sinfulness sounds at first like the ultimate in heresy, but one must consider that by Eckhart's philosophy, indeed by common logic, since all we have and are has its source in God. He shares in some way responsibility for the good and the bad. To overcome this unwelcome paradox, the Jewish religion at some time around 500 BC borrowed from the Persians the concept of Satan, a sort of malevolent shadow of the almighty God of Light, and this has come down to us as the Devil. This is at best a stopgap solution, but what we can say with confidence is that none of us ever chose to be born with frailties and faults. Although such a collaborative God as Eckhart preached may seem at first pure heresy, it is really no different from the extremely forgiving God which Jesus took pains to emphasize. Furthermore, it must be remembered that today's heresy is often tomorrow's orthodoxy, and Paul's Trinitarian theology was, and still is, heresy to the Jews. They never for a moment imagined that their stark belief in one monolithic creating divinity could ever be superseded, for was it not given by God himself to Moses? Paul's tripartite God, incorporating, as it did, a father God, a flesh and blood human-son and a vaguely defined Spirit-god, was felt to be so alien to their sacred scriptures that some of them attempted to assassinate him. As Luke tells the story, in the Great Temple in Jerusalem, the heart of Judaism and the dwelling place of God on earth, "The crowd seized him, yelling 'This is the fellow who spreads his doctrine all over the world and attacks our people, our law and this holy place .... Kill him, kill him!'" (Acts 21) It is rarely appreciated what primeval passion is unleashed when one's culturally imposed understanding of the term "God" is brought into question. Against this background, a new understanding of incarnation, as Eckhart was proposing, can hardly avoid raising emotional, even violent, reactions from those who feel that their familiar God is under threat.

As one goes deeper into all the implications of Eckhart's doctrine of spiritual union, it begins to dawn that, if he is right, oneness of this kind cannot be realised without a change of self identity which will be literally traumatic, as the psychological transition is made from self-centred to God-centred. If Eckhart's vision is to be trusted, an upheaval in traditional religion is unavoidable, for, if our complete human potential can only be fulfilled in the quest for oneness, and since nothing so extreme is seen by existing religions as their *raison d'être*, there is a sense in which Eckhart makes all religion obsolete. From an Eckhartian perspective what would normally be classified as mysticism goes from being an exceptional and exotic option to becoming a new spiritual norm. From an anthropological perspective, this development is seen as nothing less than the emergence of a new kind of human, of which Jesus is a leading example.

An individual whose life is lived in the God-centred way that Jesus manifested and Eckhart and others have preached is a different kind of human being, distinguished not morphologically (that is, by change in bodily shape) but psychologically, by change in habitual awareness, in self-awareness and in behaviour. Once this cognitive watershed has been crossed, as in the distant past a similar watershed was crossed when we went from ape to human, a new kind of human will appear, following a clear choice by every individual who thinks about these things. The choice between being self-centred or God-centred was actually there from the inception of Christianity, implicit in Paul's term *metanoia*, transformation of consciousness, but has become increasingly blurred as the stark choice preached by Paul has been watered down and dumbed down. It is probable that if a random sample of people were to be asked, "What do you think is the central message of Christianity?" most would probably settle for "Christ died for our sins" or "Do unto others as you would wish them to do unto you" or something of that kind. The astonishing religious revolution that Paul ignited and came to be identified as Christianity has lost most of its wonder and its challenge has been dulled. Quite unintentionally, Charles Darwin re-ignited it, showing it up in a new light as the chance to become a more evolved kind of human. That calls for something more than signing a baptismal register, or having someone sign for us when we are only a few days old.

Christian orthodoxy holds that Jesus co-existed with his Father from eternity and was there at the creation of the world, but Eckhart's doctrine leads clearly to the conclusion that everything that now exists in our time-space universe once existed, "before" the Big Bang. As always, "before" must be used metaphorically when dealing with a postulated timeless realm. Eckhart's novelty lies in his insistence that an integral part of human consciousness existed *in potentia* in the divine reality which is co-extensive with the *Gottheit*, about which we can otherwise say nothing. In his words,

> *God is always within the inner spark of the soul and has always been in it, eternally and with no interruption, and for man to be one with God in this requires no grace.*

Some explanation is needed of the term "grace", which in a theological context means a special action or gift. His point is that since our human essence, which is identified as the soul, is part and parcel of the timeless divine essence. It did not call for any special creative act on the part of God. There is a vital part of us that always has been God-centred and the spiritual quest consists in actualising this in our familiar 3D existence. This is a difficult concept for us three-dimensional and time-bound creatures to grasp, for we do not think naturally in terms of timelessness, and it brings with it many logical and practical questions which Eckhart does not deal with. One may perhaps gain some idea of potential existence of this kind in considering how the oak tree exists somewhere and somehow in potential in the acorn before it is actualized. Applying logic and scientific observation to our own time-line, we can be sure that each one of us must have pre-existed as a potentiality in this unimaginable realm where there was nothing but God. Our connection with this divine reality is a latency which we can choose to actualise or not, but as soon as that is said the question arises, who takes the initiative in actualising it - oneself or God? As we circle around it, awareness grows of the mystery of the oneness and of the ultimate inseparability of our true self and God.

Looking at the same mystery from a slightly different viewpoint, in *Genesis* we are told that "God made man in his own image; male and female he created them," but that inspiring statement leaves us asking what characteristics in God we have inherited or, equally intriguing, what human characteristics do we suppose that the power that created the universe actually has? By what logic can we claim to know that we are in some meaningful sense godlike or that the power which created the cosmos is human-like?

Divinisation, as Eckhart presents it, was regarded by the Church authorities at the time as heretical doctrine, but was once quite orthodox and can be found in Christian theology from the beginning. It is there unambiguously in the Second Epistle of Peter (but which in fact was not written by St Peter):

The divine power has bestowed on us everything that makes for life and true religion, enabling us to know the One who called us and come to share in the very being of God (1:3-4).

In the fourth to sixth century of the Christian Church, divinisation was preached and debated, not as an exotic footnote but as mainstream theology. The great saints and theologians whom we call the Greek Fathers wrote copiously on this theme to which they gave the term *theosis*, usually translated into English as *divinisation* [9]. Their many volumes on the theme of divinisation are sometimes summed up in Athanasius's lapidary phrase,

God became man, so that man might become God,

a theological soundbite that could have been taken straight out of any of Eckhart's sermons. A relic memory of the doctrine of *theosis* can be found in the offertory prayer of the Catholic Mass, *Deus qui humanae substantiae,* along with a beautiful symbolic action when the priest adds a drop of water to the wine in the chalice, saying aloud, "O God, who in a marvellous manner deigned to share our humanity as we share your divinity ...." Sufi writers express the same insight in various ways, most often in the metaphor of a drop of water coming from and returning to the ocean. The Hindu doctrine of Brahman and Atman makes much the same point when it teaches the doctrine of advaita (not two-ness) by comparing man's consciousness with the shared breath of the ultimate divinity Brahman.

Where Eckhart goes beyond such teachings is in drawing out the logical consequences of Athanasius's epigram, for he sees this deep indwelling of divinity as a potential that needs a human vessel to be actualised. He treats it not only as an opportunity awaiting all humans but as an opportunity for God. This unorthodox logic arises from the fact that God is incarnated within each of us but only potentially so until we consent. This is the theological core of Eckhart's revolutionary doctrine and it is stunning. In a word, the eternal timeless power that brought our time-bound universe into existence has only one opportunity to be realised on this minute scale as John Smith or Mary Brown. While He manifests in nature automatically, so to speak, without the consent of the rose, the butterfly and leaping salmon, He remains unfulfilled as the highest form of mammal, the human, without our consent. On a species level that calls for millions of individual decisions, and each is uniquely personal. Obvious though it may be, the decision cannot be made by anyone who is unaware that the choice exists and gives a totally new meaning to life. This is a God seemingly totally different from that of credal Christianity's God but, as already emphasized, it lies there as an unawakened seed in Paul's definition of the Christian as one who desires to have the same consciousness as Jesus.

It is appropriate then to ask why the doctrine of divinisation has so far dropped out of orthodox Christian belief, so as to be considered a heresy. A proper answer to that question would take us too far afield and it must suffice here to say that once Christianity went from being the deliberately chosen religion of a small and committed group of spiritual seekers and became a church for the masses, it was inevitable that this highest and most demanding of doctrines had to be reshaped into a less refined but more robust form which ordinary, mostly illiterate persons could understand and could apply in their lives. The danger is that the less refined version may over time be taken as orthodoxy, which is exactly what has happened. The problem with Christianity today is that its grand narrative defines Jesus in such a way as to make the divinisation of humans other than

Jesus anomalous, practically impossible and even heretical. This suits many nominal Christians who would prefer to worship Jesus as a flesh and blood icon, a much easier option that seeking to acquire Christ-consciousness at this deepest and transforming level.

Notes and References

1. T. S. Eliot, "The Dry Salvages" (v), *Four Quartets*. London: Faber & Faber, 1954.
2. Emmanuel Kant (1724-1804) emphasised that the words by which we label reality refer not to objects in themselves but to our limited perception of them. Our understanding is compounded from sense data, which is processed by our logical and imaginative powers and we invent a word for each new perception. Not infrequently we confuse the word with the thing in itself rather than the perception which it encodes.
3. Attribution of quotations from Eckhart has presented a problem, as they have been taken from several editions and translations, as well as from several commentators, who have not always given references. To make matters worse, the sermons are given different numberings by different translators. In this situation it has seemed best to omit most of the references to avoid cluttering of the text with unnecessary scholarship. Of the various translations and editions, there is a broad consensus today that the most authoritative is that of M. O'C. Walshe, *The Complete Mystical Works of Meister Eckhart* (NY: Crossroad Publishing Co. 2010 [3rd edn.]) It is, however, priced beyond the pocket of the average reader. There is a growing flood of popular and academic books on Eckhart, most offering valuable interpretations of his doctrine. Of these the following titles represent a sample: Oliver Davies (ed.), *Meister Eckhart: Selected Writings*. London: Penguin Classics, 1994 and *Meister Eckhart: Mystical Theologian*. London: SPCK, 2011; Cyprian Smith, *The Way of Paradox: Spiritual Life as told by Meister Eckhart*. London: Darton, Longman and Todd; 2004. Ursula Fleming, *Meister Eckhart: The Man from whom God hid Nothing*. London: Collins, 1988; Richard Woods, *Meister Eckhart: Master of Mystics*. London: Continuum, 2011; Bernard McGinn (ed.), *Meister Eckhart and the Beguine Mystics*. NY: Continuum, 1994.
4. Henry Thomas Hamblin (1872-1958) was a popular writer and speaker on spiritual matters in the mid years of the 19th century.

The quotation is from *Readings*, obtainable through the website of the Hamblin Trust or online booksellers.

5. J. Krishnamurti, *The Nature of the New Mind*. Chennai, India: Krishnamurti Foundation, 2001. p. 204.

6. The passage in question reads, "Then Jesus entered a house and again a great crowd gathered, [and] when his family heard about this, they went to take charge of him for they said, 'He is out of his mind'," (Mark 3:21-22, *New International Bible*). This is, understandably, controversial and one must always hesitate before reading the gospels as history. It is certainly possible that Jesus, speaking of mystical awareness of God, was taken by many to be deranged, but it must be kept in mind that the gospels were shaped as propaganda for Paul's new religion and the family of Jesus, as orthodox Jews, were doubtless opposed to it. Hence this incident may be an attempt by the gospel writer, or a later editor, to show them in a bad light, unable to appreciate the message of Jesus.

7. Julian of Norwich, *Showings*, "The Fifty-fourth Chapter". Trans. Edmund Colledge and James Walsh. Mahwah NJ: Paulist Press, 1978. p. 283.

8. Buber, *Thou and I*. London: Bloomsbury Academic, 2013. Was published in German in 1923 but not in English translation until 1937, with several editions since then. In it puts forward the ideal of what might be called a deep friendly relationship with God, but not the wordless intimacy of Eckhart and others that merit the term mystical.

9. Their names are a theological roll of honour, but now largely in the Greek Catholic and Greek Orthodox Churches. It includes such as Basil the Great, Gregory of Nyssa, Gregory of Nazianzen, Maximus the Confessor, Ephrem the Syrian, Cyril of Alexandria, Clement, Origen and others. See, e.g., Michael J. Christensen and Jeffrey A. Wittung (eds.), *Partakers of the Divine Nature: The History and Development of Deification in the Christian Tradition*. Grand Rapids: MI: Baker Academic, 2007.

CHAPTER 7
NEW HORIZONS

The difference I see between science and religion is difficult to put into words. To say "to be one with God" seems arrogant and flippant, but I wanted to participate in the mystery rather than walk through it like a tourist, merely observing.

Allan Sandage, Cosmologist [1]

A new axial age

The expression "axial age" was coined by the Swiss-German philosopher Karl Jaspers (1883-1969) to recognize the fact that over a period of several centuries around 500 BC, the world moved slowly from belief in many gods and goddesses to belief in a single external power. The term is very loose, for we can see monotheism arising a thousand years before that in the Egyptian worship of Aton, the sun god and in Persia in the Zoroastrian god Ahura Mazda, the origin of light and life. However, the term "Axial Age" serves a useful purpose in making the point that man's understanding of the reality we call God has evolved and, presumably, is still evolving. Early Judaism stood out from other religions for several reasons, most notably because the Jews insisted on the need for an objectively real divinity who was "holy" and "a God of truth", that is to say, a God who reflected the finest human qualities and also one who had a personal interest in the Jewish people by the fact that they recognized him, were obedient to his commandments and were thus his "unique treasure" (*Exodus* 19:5, *Malachi* 3:17). Viewed in this historical context, Christianity may be seen as a hybrid: to a primitive theory of a male sky god (the Father), permanently appeased by the sacrifice of his son (Jesus of Nazareth), has been added a spirit God (the Holy Ghost) which is to be found both in heaven and in some obscure but critical sense within the human psyche. The present work seeks to go further in arguing that a deeper understanding of "that of God within" is emerging from our recently gained information about evolution, biology and cosmology. Modern science, quite unintentionally, has provided knowledge which gives all theologies a new viewpoint from which Christianity as we have known it will come to be seen as transitional, a bridge towards a higher religion which will be at once more demanding and more fulfilling. It must be re-emphasized that the timescale of change may be in centuries and that there will be many mistakes to be made on the way as well as future revelations.

The sketch offered in these pages will probably need serious correction, but there is evidence from many quarters that a spiritual revolution of some kind is imminent. The following quotations, slightly edited, are typical of many examples that can be found.

> *A great many portents have caused us to feel, more or less confusedly, that something tremendous is taking place in the world.*
>
> Pierre Teilhard de Chardin, (*The Future of Man*, 1942)
>
> *We are living in the greatest revolution in history, a huge, spontaneous upheaval of the entire human race.*
>
> Thomas Merton, (*Conjectures of a Guilty Bystander*, 1968)
>
> *The world today is on the verge of a new axial age and a new culture. There is a feeling that we are at the end of an age.*
>
> Bede Griffiths (*A new Vision of Reality*, 1989)

Whatever this "new age and new culture" turns out to be, it must surely involve an advance in logical and empathic awareness. The whole point of this book is that it will involve not only a deeper understanding of the mysterious reality we call God, but a more meaningful relationship with it and a change in what it means to be human. With deeper God-awareness a new sense of self must emerge and then new kinds of communities, as those who seek to develop this new identity come together. If we are convinced by science that every atom in our body has its origin in the stars, which in turn can trace their origin to the primal energy that gave birth to our universe, we shall find it much easier when the time comes to take the momentous decision to let an old and "natural" self shrink and die to make way for a previously inexperienced and rather scary new kind of self. As already noted, herein lies a great "Catch 22", for how can we strive to have a kind of consciousness that we have not yet experienced? In this dilemma the crucial importance of Jesus as an exemplar becomes more apparent.

All this must deepen the need for a religion which will transcend the great faith groups whose developmental potential has been exhausted, but the idea of a global religion will call for a revolution in the thinking of most people, who take for granted that the religio-cultural blocs into which the world is now divided are, in some, way natural and permanent. This is a blind spot which afflicts even the most liberal theologians and church-men and women. The former chief rabbi of Britain, Jonathan Sacks, probably spoke for all religious leaders when he wrote of ecumenism that "while mutual friendship is desirable, and it is true that there is one divine reality and one humanity, such truths must not blind us to the fact of life "that each great faith is a universe" [2]. The contradiction in the word "universe" as he uses it goes unnoticed, for we cannot by definition have more than one universe, and it would surely be more accurate to say that each great faith believes and behaves as if it were a self-contained universe, each living in its own room in the house that is our planet, each, thinking and acting tribally, each locked into the religious insight of previous generations, and that is where some of the world's most grievous ills begin. There have been many ecumenical initiatives, invariably assuming that all religions have a common core of truth, a lowest common denominator, so to speak, on which all can agree and start building a dynamic agreement. This is, however, a convenient but naive premise. One such attempt, greatly influenced by Hindu spirituality, was promoted by the influential theosophist Annie Besant, who gave a lecture to the League of Liberal Christianity at Manchester in 1911 entitled "The Emergence of a World Religion". Her proposal was for a mighty synthesis of the best in all existing religions in "one great chord of harmony", but there is no reason to think that there is actually a common substratum on which a new religion can be built or that the conflicting identities which vastly different religions create can be subsumed into one.

A true and honest religious universe must transcend all present day divisions, and to do this it will require a common narrative and a coherent theology which does not do violence to our intelligence. It will need to appeal not only to head and heart, logic and intuition, but make them resonate together and amplify their spiritual energy. What now is needed to start on building a global family is a worldwide network of small communities, joined in a common quest for the experience of oneness with the primal reality which is our source and the source of all that exists. Some, perhaps most, will regard such an assertion as nonsense or delusion. Others who feel a need for some kind of God in their lives, but not too intrusive, will dismiss such a proposal with, "This is not religion, it is mysticism," but that is the whole point, and if Jesus were to be considered a mystic in his time, rather than a unique son of God come down from a heaven above the clouds, it would become very clear. The great challenge today is to rise above all the traditional forms of religion, not to bring them superficially together in an ecumenism without any real substance, sharing for the most part only outdated spiritual visions, some, like Judaism, from as long ago as the late Bronze Age, but rather the challenge is to bring together those who seek, however weakly or fitfully, to fulfil their human potential by developing an habitual sense of oneness with the divine, a shared will and shared perception. This is the doctrine that all the great religious teachers in Hinduism, Christianity and Islamic Sufism have preached and for which many have been persecuted and even killed by the religious leaders of their time. Such an ideal religion would not set itself against nature "to rule over every living thing that moves upon the earth", as God commands in the Book of Genesis, but would find divinity in the natural world. In Eckhart's words,

> *The most trivial thing perceived in God. A flower for example as espied in God would be a thing more perfect than the universe.* [3]

The phrase "perceived in God" is the key. It is an unnatural mode of consciousness for humans at our present stage of evolution, and the core theme of the present work is that developing it, is the task of true religion today. It is largely undeveloped because the essence of Christianity, acquiring Christ-consciousness, is seen through the distorting lens of the Nicene Creed.

A new creation story

It would be far too simple to say that we only need a "scientific" theology to resolve the religious crisis, if only because the foundations of science are themselves being shaken, and the rebuilding of science on new principles is becoming urgent. It will be a science of being (ontology) and of knowing (epistemology), for science is now asking radical questions about how reality is to be defined and recognized, how we know and how we can be certain. A new kind of science is being forced into birth because quantum physics has to deal with patterns of energy, not the "hard, solid, massy, unbreakable" particles of Isaac Newton's science, and, strange as it may seem, scientists have no clear idea of what energy actually is, only of its physical effects. The Nobel laureate Richard Feynman made this point explicitly in his widely acclaimed *Lectures on Physics*, "It is important to realise that in physics today we have no knowledge of what energy is [4]." We need therefore a deeper understanding of the reality that underlies chemical, electrical, magnetic, heat and light energy and how all these are related to the energy of motion, as highlighted below. Two fundamental questions are now arising: (i) What is it that remains invariant in all the transformations of energy and, (ii) Is the energy of consciousness part of this rich intellectual tapestry? We know that consciousness, and in particular will, is a form of energy, for a willed intention is necessary to move any part of our body. Lifting a mug of coffee is achieved by a train of electro-chemical muscular events, but nothing happens until I will it to happen. There can be no doubt that the energy of consciousness can influence events of this kind and on this scale but the great scientific bogey which rattles its chains behind a curtain of denial is the question of whether or not a greater consciousness can influence things on a larger scale and it must be said that there is no logical reason why not. In principle it is possible, but as things stand at present, religion says it happens and most scientists either say it cannot happen or ignore the logic because they cannot face the conclusions to which it leads. There are a good few famous exceptions to this, including Arthur Eddington, James Jeans, David Bohm, Freeman Dyson and Max Planck, the founder of quantum physics, who is forthright in his belief and worth quoting here for that reason:

> *As a man who has devoted his whole life to the most clear-headed science, the study of matter, I can tell you that there is no matter as such! Matter originates and exists only by the virtue of a force which brings the particles of the atom to vibration and holds this most minute solar system of the atom together .... We must assume behind this force the existence of a conscious and intelligent Spirit. This Spirit is the matrix of matter.* [5]

The God-problem did not trouble the founders of science, many of whom were very religious individuals, for they were content to postulate an unknown first cause and leave it at that. Isaac Newton was very typical when he wrote, "Does it not appear from Phenomena that there is a Being incorporeal, living, intelligent, omnipresent, who in infinite Space, as it were in his Sensory, sees the things themselves intimately ... Of which things the Images only carried through the Organs of Sense into our little Sensoriums are seen and beheld by that which in us perceives and thinks [6]." In more modern English, this might be paraphrased, "Logic tells us that there must be a first cause, but all we know about it is what our limited senses allow us to know."

In its early period science as we now know it was called natural philosophy, that is to say, knowledge obtained by examining nature and, in particular, by measuring it. The emerging new science could be called post-natural or trans-natural philosophy. Thanks to marvellous advances in telescopy we now know that our universe came into existence 13.7 billion years ago and with this knowledge science leaps forward; from astronomy, which is the observation of a fixed universe of stars, into cosmology, which is a historical account of the cosmos, and from there into cosmogony, which is the theory of cosmic origin - that is to say, of creation. Thus the most fascinating science of our time is, by definition, outside of observational proof. However, we can gain some minimal idea of what is at issue from the following figure, which the labels make more or less self-explanatory. Just after the Big Bang point, when time and our 3D universe came into existence, the diagram shows a small triangle, labelled "Planck domain". This represents an unimaginably small volume of space, billions of billions times smaller than a speck of flour, which came into existence billionths of a second after the Big Bang, and it marks the boundary of science's present knowledge. Physicists have no idea of the "structure" of energy during this unimaginably brief period of expansion, and this is why they tend to draw a line here in their theorizing and talk in a hand-waving way about "quantum foam". The space above the Big Bang point, represented as a wedge converging on this point, indicates rather crudely a timeless universe from which emerged our familiar time-bound cosmos, normally taken to be the entire universe. The timeless universe may be identified with the scientific concept of hyperspace and is a crude attempt to indicate a timeless realm of more than three dimensions. At the point which marks the Big Bang both time and space came into existence.

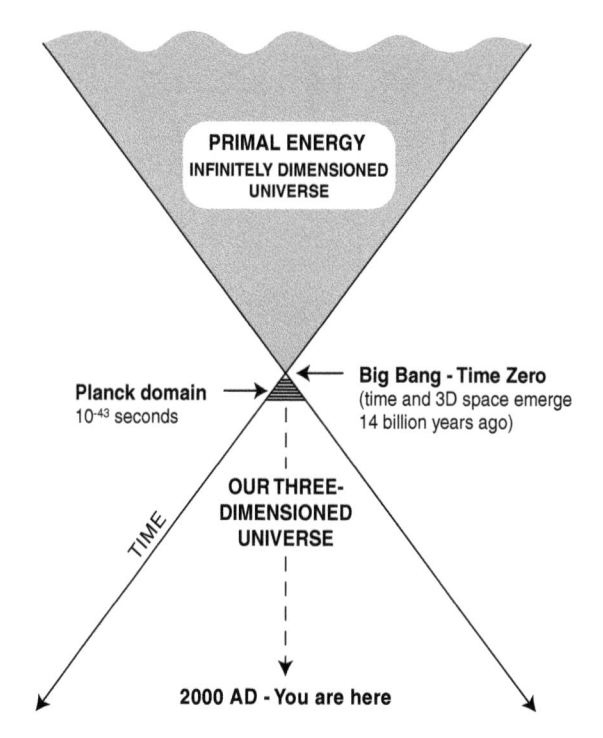

```
                    PRIMAL ENERGY
                 INFINITELY DIMENSIONED
                       UNIVERSE


                                    Big Bang - Time Zero
     Planck domain                  (time and 3D space emerge
     10⁻⁴³ seconds                  14 billion years ago)

                    OUR THREE-
                    DIMENSIONED
                     UNIVERSE


                  2000 AD - You are here
```

Figure 1   The emergence of our universe of space and time

It will be noted how compatible this is with Eckhart's concept of the infinite, eternal and timeless Godhead. The difficulties of representing hyperspace visually at all, let alone on the two-dimensional surface of a page, need hardly be emphasized, and for practical purposes it is probably better to consider our 3D universe as dissolved invisibly in an infinitely dimensioned reality, like salt in brine, from which it may be precipitated by deliberate action.

Figure 2 below is a *jeu d'esprit* of the eminent physicist John Wheeler and shows the current stage of our evolving planet earth, since it began life as a ball of hot and molten rock. It illustrates how the emergence of humanity has given consciousness to the universe - represented as the large "U" - creating what the Russian geochemist Vladimir Vernadsky and the palaeontologist Teilhard de Chardin called the "*noosphere*", in parallel with the biosphere and atmosphere. It is this frail skin of evolving consciousness which gives meaning not only to the planet but to our existence.

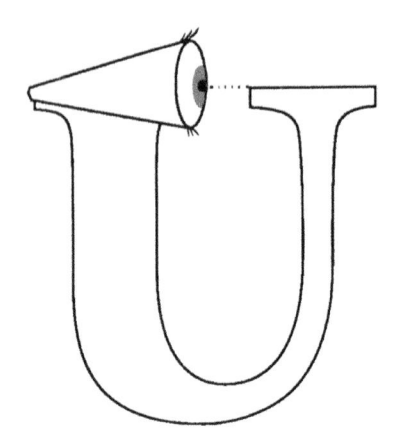

Figure 2 The universe becomes self-conscious

Both these diagrams can be contrasted with the following, which is a representation of a world view from two thousand years ago. It is a composite made up from various statements about the nature of heaven and earth in the Old and New Testaments. It is as different from the normal person's current understanding of the universe, as that is different from the 3D cosmos within a timeless universe, that is being revealed by science.

Figure 3 The biblical world view

Odd as it may appear to the modern mind, it is by no means illogical, for if rain comes down from above, it is not unreasonable to hypothesize the existence of a firmament of water between heaven and earth. This picture would have been the vaguely imagined world view of Jesus and his contemporaries, thus making the story of his bodily ascent into heaven through a cloud - which conveniently "removed him from the disciples' sight" (Acts 1:9) - perfectly believable. The Greek "scientific" model of the cosmos, it is worth noting, was quite different from this commonsense world view, locating the earth at the centre of concentric revolving crystal spheres which carried the stars. It is of interest that mediaeval diagrams of this Russian doll kind of universe often located the ultimate centre of the universe in Jerusalem. How this Middle Eastern Stone Age hill fortification became the "Holy City" for three of the world's great religions is a fascinating story and a sad commentary on man's tribal consciousness.

Neurotheology

On a quite different scientific frontier, studies of the brain and the nervous system and microbiology are generating new understanding of the brain and of consciousness, some of which bears directly on spirituality. Two only of the new discoveries will be treated here, but this should be sufficient to show how this area of science is opening up new horizons in theology. Perhaps the most important discovery is that humans have the power to shape the brain by systematic attempts to acquire certain skills. The best known example of this is an experimental study which was done on London taxi drivers who had spent two or three years learning how to go from any part of the city to any other part most effectively, in order to qualify for a licence, after passing a rigorous examination, appropriately called "The Knowledge". The study is recounted in many popular books [7]. What the researchers found, to their surprise, was that the newly qualified drivers had expanded a particular part of the brain, the hippocampus, as a consequence of their learning and this became a quasi-permanent neural structure. Later research showed that other parts of the brain changed similarly in response to directed learning, leading to the more general conclusion that, within limits, we can create the kind of brain required to produce the kind consciousness that we want, if we are prepared to work at it. This raises the question, what kind of habitual consciousness do we want? A pianist or darts player will after hundreds or thousands of hours of practice, change the shape and function of their brain to produce a clearly required skill. Where once the pianist struggled with five finger exercises, he or she can eventually play complex arpeggios without effort or thought, because the neural structures required to make this happen have developed in response to their repeated attempts. The skill is never entirely lost, although it may diminish without practice. The spiritual seeker has a far less definable "skill" to aim for and a poorly understood programme of action that will reliably produce it, but such a programme, or "way", will turn out to be the implicit definition of a new religion.

This potential for reconstructing the brain has been given the names *neurogenesis* or *neuroplasticity*. In a religious context the significance of this discovery is that the transformation of consciousness by which essential Christianity is, or should be, defined must issue from a change in normal brain structure. This structure is well developed in those rare individuals that we call saints but rudimentary in the normal person. Once we have a strong desire to "know God" and have a reliable method of achieving that state, persistent application of it will eventually create the part of the brain necessary to generate a sense of God, just as the olfactory lobe generates the sense of smell. Perhaps "generate" is not the best word to apply to the new and mysterious kind of consciousness that emerges from the unfocused striving which several mystical writers identify as simply "naked intent". In some incomprehensible way our striving, the interaction of knower and known, creates God in a mysterious divine-human mode: in seeking to know God we make God happen, or God makes himself happen through us. We are here in uncharted waters, calling for a new vocabulary and new categories. Further comment will be reserved for a later section. In this simplest of expositions, it must be noted that there are several immediate snags. Firstly, one must be sure that the desire to know God is not just a passing mood and at base self-centred, for it will eventually have to be purchased at the cost of self, a painful handover, and secondly, we must find an effective method from among the many which are on offer in what has been called the spiritual market place. The expression is all too accurate, for many self-promoting spiritual gurus are in it for love of profit rather than love of truth.

A fundamental problem in the spiritual quest arises from the fact that we do not know what it feels like to have habitual and natural God-awareness. We may have had occasional peak experiences that gave a brief taste of a higher and purer consciousness, but living in the Presence is certainly not living continuously on an emotional high. We do not know how it feels to be trans-human and thus have no clear goal to aim for and so we experience only what Emerson called the "divine discontent." Even so, once we are aware of something lacking and of a definite wish to have it, we are on the rails and travelling in the right direction. Yet another obstacle arises from lack of a community to support, guide and correct us. One can, of course, still grow spiritually without a community, and a period of solitary struggle is probably an essential part of the journey, but without a community to which we give and from which we take and by which we are nourished, tested and shaped, there is grave danger that spirituality will insensibly become a refined form of selfishness or curiosity-seeking rather than a God-centred state. Such communities will have to be "in the world but not of it" and thus of necessity will have to create an interface with it, while keeping much of the world out. There will also need to be an agreed learning programme, which will call for a total rethink of education.

The second finding of neurology calling for mention is the discovery in the 1990's of mirror neurons in the brain, so-called because they fire automatically in sympathy with other people's emotions, such as fear, excitement or disgust. The responder does not even need to know the person with whom their brain is resonating in empathy. Mirror neurons also exist in the higher primates and sometimes dramatically so in dogs, which will come as no surprise to those who have experienced their dog's sympathy. The full impact of mirror neurons on both neurology and psychology has yet to be appreciated, but many believe that it is a revolution in waiting. Indeed, one of the most prominent workers in this field, V. S. Ramachandran [8], has gone so far as to claim that "mirror neurons will do for psychology what DNA did for biology." This "new philosophy", as he called it, was the theme of his 2003 BBC Reith Lectures.

Mirror neurons are important in religion, for they provide empirical evidence that we are linked into a single organism through shared communication at the neuronal level. This is a truth recognized from the beginning by Christianity in the concept of "the body of Christ" and the image of a vine and branches in John's gospel. In the *Go-between God*, Bishop John Vincent Taylor has a striking passage on the exceptional empathy that should define the Christian and trans-Christian community, quoted here in slightly abbreviated form:

> *Like a peal of bells the word* 'allelon' *– "one another" – rings through the pages of the New Testament. "Accept one another"* – allelon – *Serve one another* – allelon – *confess your sins to one another, forgive one another, teach and admonish one another, comfort one another and build each other up, bear one another's burdens and love one another.* [9]

Concluding this brief foray into neurotheology, it is worth mentioning that researchers seeking to identify the parts of the brain which are associated with spiritual or meditative awareness have located it largely in the prefrontal cortex, sometimes called "the brain of the brain", and in the rear parietal lobes. In the first instance, as a meditative state deepens, the prefrontal cortex switches off and mental activity of an analytical or imaginative nature dies down. This suggests strongly that God-awareness is not so much mindfulness as mindlessness, as it comes with deliberate closing down of mental activity. The mindlessness of the meditative state, which is the "unknowing" of the mediaeval classic "*The Cloud of Unknowing*", an anonymous work of Christian mysticism, is on the surface at least, the opposite of the practice of mindfulness as taught by many contemporary guides, as for instance Eckhart Tolle and the Buddhist Thich Nhat Hanh and this is a source of confusion that calls for clarification. The theological conclusions that may be drawn at this stage from research into neurogenesis are by no means clear, but point to a paradoxical conclusion. It seems that the highest function of human intelligence may now be to disable itself in order for a totally new kind of a-logical and imageless consciousness to emerge. Our proudest evolutionary achievement to date may be, ironically, an intellectual scaffolding that must now be dismantled to reveal within it a new kind of intelligence which looks at first to be a deliberate ignorance. It seems to share the kind of selflessness that is associated with being in love, when the normal boundary between self and other seem to be magically dissolved. In this happy state doing something for the other is indistinguishable from doing it for oneself.

Notes and References

1. Quoted in William A. Durbin, *Negotiating the Boundaries of Science and Religion II*. In PDF. Sandage was Hubble's successor at the Palomar Observatory and is widely credited with establishing the science of observational cosmology.
2. Jonathan Sacks, "Credo," *The Times*, October 12, 2002.
3. Quoted in T. D. Suzuki, *Mysticism: Christian and Buddhist*. London: Routledge, 2002. p. 5. Suzuki is a highly regarded commentator in this field, but in trying to show the hidden Buddhist principles in Christian mysticism, (not the other way round), he glosses over the fact that Christians seek a relationship with God. Zen has no space for a creating God and would be destructured if one were to be put in even as a footnote. By contrast, without

a God at its centre, Christian mysticism would hardly be distinguishable from transcendental meditation.
4. *The Feynman Lectures*. NY: Basic Books, (2010). Vol. 1 4-1.[1964].
5. In a speech given at Florence in 1944, *Das Wesen der Materie (The Nature of Matter)*.
6. Isaac Newton, *Opticks*, 1717, Query 28.
7. See, e.g., Sharon Begley, *The Plastic Mind: New Science Reveals Our Extraordinary Potential to Transform Ourselves* (London: Constable, 2009), Susan Greenfield, *Mind Change: How Digital Technologies are Leaving their Mark on our Brains* (London: Random House, 2015) and Norman Doidge, *The Brain that Changes Itself*. Penguin, 2008. The original research is in E. A. Maguire, et al. "Navigation-related structural change in the hippocampi of taxi drivers", *Proceedings of the National Academy of Science, USA* 97 (2000: 4398-4403).
8. See, e.g., *The Tell Tale Brain: Unlocking the Mystery of Human Nature*. London: Windmill Books, 2012 and his earlier, best-selling *Phantoms in the Brain: Human Nature and the Architecture of the Mind*. London: Fourth Estate, 1999.
9. John V. Taylor, *The Go-between God*. London: SCM Press, 1989. p. 126. First published in 1972, this is the thirteenth impression.

CHAPTER 8
SEEKING THE REAL "ME"

We are in the twilight of the modern self and face an unknown future where ethnic, religious and national identities become blurred in a global civilization.
　　　　　　　　　　Walter Truett Anderson. *The Future of the Self* [1]

The evolving self

Clear evidence for the emergence of self-awareness in the human species can be traced back to the late Ice Age with the appearance of Cro-magnon man, which the palaeontologist Ian Tattersall has called an "explosion" in human evolution [2]. Using the same metaphor, Jesus's identification of his self with the divine reality may be seen as a second explosion and we are now on the verge of a third explosion, when the flood of new knowledge, which began with the scientific revolution, is merging with spiritual intelligence to create a new sense of human identity. The changes in brain structure which enabled our forebears to advance from herd-consciousness to self-consciousness were first sketched out in 1976 by the psycho-historian Julian Jaynes in his classic work *The Origin of Consciousness in the Breakdown of the Bicameral Mind*. Jaynes argued that about three thousand years ago our ancestors, in the region of Greece and the Middle East, underwent a fundamental change of consciousness that laid the foundation for the modern concept of the independent self. Over a period of centuries, they went from a situation in which members of the group thought and felt passively like the group to one in which they started to regard themselves as individuals, with the ability to think and make decisions independently. Much later, developing and exercising this new ability came to be felt as a moral responsibility, with the American Constitution in 1788 marking a milestone in the new "self-awareness". Jaynes described the in-between state, as a kind of schizophrenia - that is, split consciousness - and provides many examples from ancient literature and pictorial records to support his thesis. A clear break with unselfconscious humans came in ancient Greece, a strong contributory factor being a new form of social structure, the democratic city state. At the entrance to the temple of Apollo at Delphi, the most important in Greece, was inscribed Gnothi seauton, that is, "Know Thyself", which summed up the religious force of this new discovery of the independent self.

It was a discovery that Greek philosophers and dramatists cherished and celebrated and the legend was that it was a message brought down from heaven by the god Apollo himself. It need hardly be said, that this awareness of self-awareness, which was both a gift and a moral imperative, marked an evolutionary step change, the passage from the childhood to the adulthood of man.

The lack, even of a word for 'self' in other languages is nowhere so marked as in the gospel passage where Jesus makes the critical pronouncement that one must lose one's old self to find the new self. One wonders what Jesus actually said in Aramaic, which probably did not have a word for 'self', but the Greek of the gospel (Mark 8:35) *psychen autou* resists precise translation. One version of the New Testament renders it as "true self" (*New English Bible*), another simply as "life" (*Revised Standard Version*), and another as "soul" (*New International Version*). This ambiguity makes it difficult to get to the heart of Eckhart's message, and indeed to Paul's call for *metanoia*. All that can be said is that one who truly knows God has found a new self and cast off the old one.

The new self will be consciously aware of being a member of a new kind of civilisation, a member of a global family as yet struggling to be born. The word *civilisation* is related to the Latin *civis*, meaning a city dweller, and is the opposite of barbarous or heathen, the latter meaning literally a heath-dweller. "Civilisation," says Jaynes, "is the art of living in towns of such size that everyone does not know everyone else." [3] Today we in the West never think of living in a city as being an effort, let alone an art, but history is now repeating itself on a much grander scale, forcing us to develop a new kind of transnational and trans-ethnic consciousness for the survival of the planet. This will inevitably call for the creation of new kinds of social structure. The challenge now is to create a global family from a planet divided into national, linguistic and religious groups, which do not know each other and whose "natural" instinct is not cooperation and mutual understanding but, rather, suspicion, antagonism, exploitation and even predation. Just as man's survival once depended on moving from a hunting to a nomadic-pastoral and then to a settled agricultural way of life, before becoming civilized - that is to say, city-ized and town-ized - planetary survival now depends on becoming globe-ized. Acquiring a true global identity will call for a higher kind of empathy than we would now consider normal, which in turn will call for learning more about other cultures, not just incidentally, through magazine articles and TV documentaries, but through a specially designed and systematic programme of education. There is no quick fix: however long the quest may be, it can only come about by individuals making the decision to embark on the great adventure of acquiring a new sensitivity, a change so radical that it might be regarded as creating a new self. The global imperative will call for an appropriate macrostructure, probably a sort of "shadow UN", but more immediately there will be need for a new microstructure, most obviously local "families", along lines that will be taken up below.

A strong sense of self was not possible until mirrors came into common use and writing was invented. Mirrors enabled our foreparents to stand back and observe themselves as objects, while seeing our thoughts on the page enables us to inspect them and treat them as something separate from the observing "me". Slowly this sense of having a core "me" and an independent self with its own values has grown until it has become, in most parts of the world, a new norm. It is, however, very much a Western phenomenon, preached with religious fervour during the period of the Enlightenment in the eighteenth century. It is epitomised in Kant's phrase, *Aude sapere*, which may be loosely translated as "Dare to think for yourself", and later in the well known line of the Victorian poet W. E. Henley, "I am the master of my fate, I am the captain of my soul." It is hard to imagine such a thought being uttered by someone who is illiterate. Today we face the challenge of acquiring a new literacy that will be required in the creation of a new sense of self, at once clearly independent, with innate ego-strength but with a sense of total dependence on the invisible reality that we call God. That is the dynamic paradox at the heart of the new human.

Not everyone, by any means, is in favour of a society made up of strong and independent selves, most obviously so the governing class and the advertising industry. For them a free-thinking population constitutes a threat to their political power and potential for financial exploitation. In 2002 the BBC screened a landmark documentary series entitled *The Century of the Self*, which focused on the part played by Edward Bernays (coincidentally, Freud's nephew) in providing politicians and the marketing industry with the tools to control the independent self for their own nefarious purposes. It should be required viewing for every high school student. Bernays' main publication was *Propaganda*, (1928), which had a great influence on Joseph Goebbels, particularly in showing how "the big lie" can be used to numb our logical sense and moral judgement. Bernays' thesis was that anyone who understands the psychological processes which lead to decision-making - usually more emotional than logical - can shape the public's behaviour and in a quite literal sense control the public mind. Bernays did not see this as an abstract theory but as a kind of perverse crusade in a new religion of consumerism. In the words of his business partner, Paul Mazur, "We must shift America from a 'needs culture' to a 'desires culture'. People must be trained to desire, to want new things, even before the old have been entirely consumed. We must shape a new mentality." [4]

George Orwell was among the few who could clearly see how this was being done by totalitarian governments in the 1930's and 1940's and his fictionalised warnings in *Animal Farm* and *1984* are as relevant today as then, indeed more relevant. At the very least, ordinary citizens should be aware of the main techniques by which their minds are being controlled, the overarching one being to stimulate uncritical, knee-jerk response from emotions arising from the primitive part of the brain in order to over-ride logical thinking, which arises from the highest part of the brain. In this respect, advertisers and very often politicians are setting back evolutionary progress and returning us to a state where we act not coolly and rationally but "instinctively", that is to say, by automatic response from what might be called our lower or animal brain. It hardly needs to be said how fatal this must be to democratic government, but its deeper effects on society are more obviously seen in the use of mind control by the marketing and advertising industry. Rarely do we ever become aware of the way in which our emotions are being manipulated by television commercials and advertising more generally. In this respect it should be pointed out that the marketing industry has become a key part of the alternative quasi-religion of consumerism, a word which did not exist fifty years ago. Consumerism, often called "retail therapy" in a quite serious way, replaces the Christian culture of past centuries and stands morality on its head, making selfishness and covetousness into virtues. As Gordon Gekko, the fictional hero of the cult film *Wall Street*, put it in a memorable nutshell, "Greed, for want of a better name, is good." Margaret Thatcher put it less controversially in saying "There's nothing wrong with profit," but there is certainly something wrong with making profit the centre of one's life and of life in general. The greatest cause for concern in all this is the factor which Bernays most emphasized, that the average individual is completely oblivious to the way that advertisers and politicians push and pull the levers in our brains, so to speak, for their own nefarious purposes and silently steal critical elements of what we think of as our inviolable self.

A different but equally worrying threat to the healthy independent self has arisen in the last thirty or forty years from information technology. It comes from different directions, but most obviously from the amount of time that individuals now spend online, particularly involved in so-called social media. Much has been written about this shift in social behaviour and all that needs to be mentioned here is that in the UK and many other countries, a large and increasing proportion of the population spends a large part of every day online, listening to music, endlessly browsing but mostly gossiping and exchanging trivial information. An in-depth July 2017 Nielsen poll in America revealed the extent to which IT has taken over our lives, especially with the so-called 'millennials', whom the dictionary defines as the generation reaching young adulthood around the turn of the twentieth century. The United States no doubt leads the way in this, with the UK a close second, but there can be little doubt that the rest of the world is following. The general conclusion to be drawn from the Nielsen data, which is replicated in similar polls in the UK is that for many the "virtual world" is becoming the real reality. The average teenager spends over half his or her waking life interacting with media, at a screen, watching television, computer, tablet or smart phone, gaming with a console, using email, listening to radio or to "streamed" music. They are, in effect, living within a technological matrix without any awareness of the fact, and in addition to the psychological manipulation just mentioned, an even more alarming behind-the-scenes-force is silently at work. Because the main channels of information are owned by a small number of individuals with unstated agendas, they can, and certainly do, act as gatekeepers for the information we are allowed to receive. In America some 90% of television programming is controlled by just six giant media. Only if one takes the trouble to identify the individuals who own the newspapers and TV channels can one become aware of their political or economic agenda [5].

At another level entirely is the opportunity opened up by the anonymity of the Internet to invent Web personae. Sherry Turkle, a recognized authority in this field, puts this forward in both a positive and negative light. On the one hand it offers, or so she argues, the potential to create a personality that society accepts as real but which we have invented. On the other hand, in creating several such artificial selves, the experimenter risks a growing uncertainty about who is the "real me" [6]. This "existential angst", as Jean-Paul Sartre called it is no longer confined to the philosophically minded but threatens a whole society. The situation was summed up some years ago by a *New Yorker* cartoon in which two dogs are seen sitting in front of computer screens, one of them typing to the other, "and the great thing is that no one knows I'm a dog", completely oblivious, of course, to the fact that it knows nothing of the "person" with whom it is building up a so-called relationship.

All this has gone along with the collapse of Christian culture in the West. Within a century Europe has changed from a situation where the great majority of people would identify themselves as Christians, whether or not they went to church, to one in which churches are now virtually empty, thousands have been sold off (some to be turned into mosques) and more than half the population of Britain declare themselves as non-religious. As the new quasi-religions of materialism and scientism have grown, the eternal questions of self and self-fulfilment and the meaning of existence have reappeared in a new form. These were adequately answered within the framework of the Christian narrative in the West. The meaning of life and of my life could be taken for granted and summed up in a few simple words, as in the shorter Catholic Catechism, "God made me to know Him, love Him and serve Him in this life and to be happy with Him forever in the next." Now that the old God has been banished from literate society, and certainly from scientific society, answers to these vital questions about the self and its essential value are typically sought in the psychotherapist's consulting room and the journals of clinical psychology. Often the origin of the depressive and confused feelings of patients is traced to the lack of a spiritual dimension in their life. It is difficult for the psychotherapist to be a healer in these cases without bringing in the need for belief in a higher power, now that society has largely rejected the conventional God of Judaeo-Christianity but left a God-shaped hole in life. It is of more than passing interest that 'Alcoholics Anonymous' attempts to fill it for its agnostic members by requiring them to seek help from an undefined power or, as they put it, simply "God as you understand Him."

Without going so far, the recognition by psychologists of a spiritual dimension as a necessary element in mental health is something of a revolution, since the psychological disciplines have long attempted to maintain scientific status by excluding God and anything remotely resembling spirituality from their research. The beginnings of this new and, it should be said, still controversial development can be traced back to several individuals, most notably Carl Jung in Europe and the American Abraham Maslow's theory of human needs first published in book form in his *Motivation and Personality* in 1954. Maslow is in many ways the more interesting, free of the sort of counter-mythology that mars Jung's genuine insights and fully consonant with a theory of human evolution. He was for many years the doyen of American psychotherapists, the driving principle of his teaching being that mental health was not just freedom from neuroses but involved satisfying a hierarchy of needs, the highest in rank being a strong sense of self, of self-value and of one's place in the world. His innovation was to rank these needs in order of urgency, which he represented as a triangle divided into layers, with man's animal instincts at the base and the urge to "self-actualisation" at the peak. This simple and almost commonsense approach has turned out, however, to be a psychological and religious 'tar baby', as the implications of "self-actualisation" started to unfold.

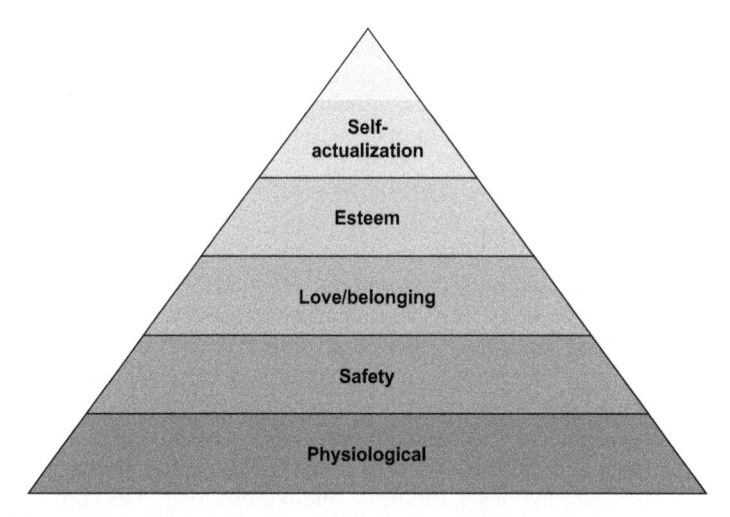

Figure 4 Maslow's hierarchy of needs, more basic at the bottom

The labels used here are taken from various models that Maslow tried out over a period of some thirty years, as new insight came to him. He did not put his hierarchy of human needs forward specifically as a theory of human evolution, but it is clear that the sequence in which he labelled them follows an evolutionary trajectory, from animal to human and, if the thesis of the present book is accepted, to something beyond human as we have known it. The model has a natural structure arising from the fact that the lowest needs in the triangle must be satisfied before attempting to meet those above. Maslow's theory has provided grist for innumerable articles and books on the broad theme of human needs and this is without doubt because of its protean nature. Almost everyone who meets this hierarchical and dynamic model of the self will immediately see where it could be improved or extended. It is thus an excellent starting point for exploration into the nature of the self.

What is of particular interest in Maslow's model, in the present context of spiritual evolution, is that from its introduction in 1943 the continuous refinements which he made were mostly at the level of what he initially called "self-actualisation". Increasingly he came to see "constant betterment" as a genuine survival need if we are to become fully human and re-labelled it as "self-transcendence". Where once our basic survival needs were seen to be the strictly animal requirements of food, sex and shelter, Maslow's emphasis slowly shifted as he came to see a spiritualised self as peculiarly human. Without this desire for spiritual satisfaction we cannot be fully human. In his last book, *Farther Reaches of Human Nature*, published posthumously, he argued explicitly that the top level of the hierarchical model, now clearly labelled *self-transcendence*, "refers to the very highest and most inclusive or holistic levels of human consciousness" and to awareness of our connection to "other species, to nature and to the cosmos."

The "I" that meets God

We tend to think of the self as unitary, easily identifiable, spatially bounded by our body and centred more precisely in our brain, where thinking take place. The least reflection, however, reveals how simplistic this assumption is. The mere fact that we can think of improving the self and make decisions about how to do it implies that there is some other entity, logically another kind of self, that does the planning and the execution. In the field of cognitive psychology and particularly hypnosis, the term "hidden observer" has come to be used to mark the fact, shown many times experimentally, that a hypnotised subject will not obey the hypnotist's commands when instructed to do something that would offend his or her moral code. In this (and in other conflicting situations) a separate and somehow a higher and truer self seems to take over. First noted by Ernest Hilgard in 1977 [7], the hidden observer phenomenon remains a source of puzzlement and controversy. Hilgard himself expressed surprise that what began as an ad hoc and commonsense answer to a simple question (i.e., whether or not the hypnotist could, make the subject behave immorally) was to ramify into so many alternative theories. The hidden observer was, he wrote later, "initially intended merely as a conventional label for the information source capable of a high level of cognitive functioning not consciously experienced by the hypnotised person [8]." The implications of this discovery go far beyond hypnotherapy and as one goes deeper into the issues that spin off, there grows a suspicion that a radically new theory of consciousness may be needed to explain all the related insights now appearing in fields as wide apart as evolutionary zoology and theology. A major step in this direction was made in the 1960's by the neuroscientist Paul MacLean with his concept of the triune brain [9], the significance of which is that the human brain can be seen as three brains, almost literally piled on each other as consciousness advanced from reptilian to mammalian to human. This is shown in the following diagram [10].

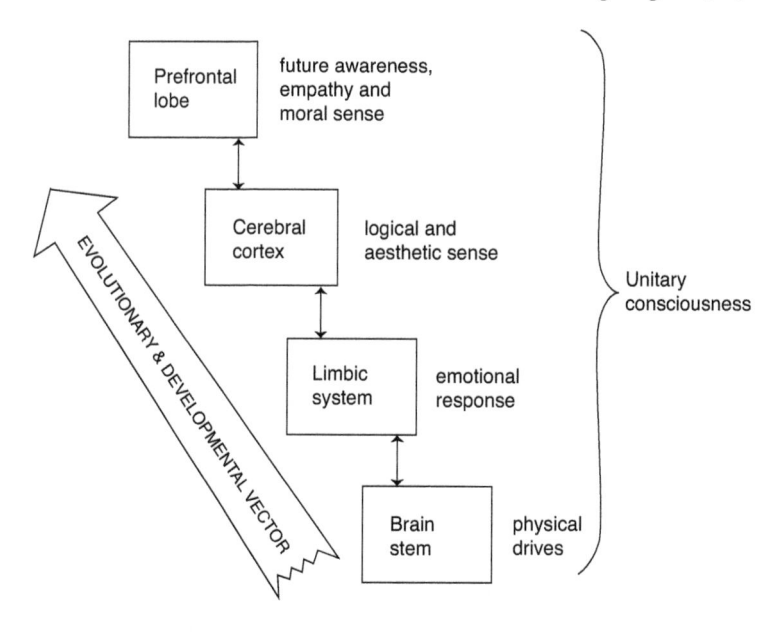

Figure 5 Our four level brain

One important point of this model is that in generating different kinds of consciousness each of the three substructures constitutes a semi-independent self and these are often in conflict with one another. St Paul's personal statement of this state of affairs in his letter to the Romans rings painfully true to any spiritual seeker, "The good that I want to do I don't do, and the bad that I don't want to do, I find myself doing." The intriguing question now arising is whether or not a fourth "spiritual" brain needs now to be added to the existing three brains in order to fulfil our human destiny or, alternatively, can the hoped-for effect be achieved by a rearrangement of existing functions? To pursue this line of enquiry would take the reader too far away from the main theme but it should be again emphasized that knowing God in the unmediated sense that Rahner sought and mystics have achieved, involves the disabling of what until now we have regarded as the highest brain function.

Some "out-of-the-box thinking" now seems to be required and there is reason to believe that the answer may lie in the most primitive component of the brain, a structure we share with the lowest forms of animal life and which is indeed so primitive that it is not normally regarded as part of the brain. This is the reticular formation, located below the brain in the brain stem, the function of which is, loosely speaking, to switch on the brain by giving attention to something in the environment. Different things turn it on. Its function can be seen, for instance, in a mother who is alerted to the slightest noise made by her sleeping child in another room, which others would not hear. What we are alerted to is in some respects a measure of how human we are and, as we become more human, this primitive faculty comes into play in recognizing significances. What we *feel* as significant cannot be argued against: we just know that this information is important and we give it our attention. At a lower biological level this reflex function can be seen quite dramatically. A classical paper in neurology entitled "What the frog's eye tells the frog's brain [11]" explains how the retina of a particular kind of frog is so structured that it sees primarily movement rather than shapes or colour, and when an insect crosses its field of vision, its tongue flicks out to catch it automatically, without any decision called for. With this sort of background knowledge the philosopher and theologian may work together to better understand what is happening in the brain when we are attentive to God and, in some limited sense, to determine what may be possible to make such attention a reflexive action. God awareness may also originate as a function of the so-called "split brain", some evidence for which will be provided later. As many great saints have said, the whole world speaks to them of God, but this is not a normal human reaction and if we are not one of those particularly blessed individuals, it will not come naturally but must be learned. From this perspective the whole point of religion is now seen to be how to learn it. The dividing line is not between those who have this gift and those who do not have it, but between those who do not have it and those who want it. However faint it may at first be, this desire to know God is the great gift. With it we can move on to become a new kind of human, without it we are helpless to grow in this way. However, as will be seen, having or acquiring such God-awareness is only the first stage in the great transformation. The challenge of *metanoia* is taking the decision to dissolve and lose what we would normally consider to be our very own and inviolable self.

These considerations lead back to the question of multiple selfs and the human need to find the true self, to know "who I am". As well as the hidden observer, there is evidence for the existence of several kinds of consciousness co-existing in obscure relationships, each of which seems to arise from a semi-independent self. This is seen most dramatically in the so-called "alien hand syndrome", when one hand does things that are unintended by the person suffering from this mental disorder. Typically, it will undo buttons that the other hand has just done up, but often can place the sufferer in socially embarrassing situations [12]. This can be partly, but by no means completely, explained from the figure above, where an animal self and an intelligent/spiritual self can be seen as issuing naturally from the two "top" brains, each having partial control of our behaviour. A quite different kind of self can be seen in Socrates' conviction, which came from his personal experience, that there exists a spirit guide, seemingly both integral with and separate from his mind, which warns and advises wordlessly. This ambivalent entity, which he called his *Daimon* (or *Daemon*), is common in Stoic teaching and more particularly in that of Epictetus. It is also found in Catholic Christianity in the form of the Guardian Angel, but there it is a completely independent entity and part of a complex mythology of angels who function as divine messengers. This grey area of theology conceals very important questions, of which the most important concern the nature and limit of freewill and the direct action of God in our lives.

As one explores these ramifying questions about what constitutes the real me, what once seemed so solid and obvious can easily take on the confusion of a hall of mirrors, and with infinite regress, neatly summed up by Alan Watts,

What I'd like to see is the I that knows
When I know that I know that I know.

If we can find what exactly is doing the knowing, we have surely found the real me, from which arises the startling conclusion that it is actually God knowing himself through me. To attempt a bold but risky conclusion, my true self is what I allow God to know of me. It is risky because it plunges us into the age-old theological conundrum of nature and grace or, expressed as a simple question, who takes the initiative - God or me?

Notes and References

1. Walter Truett Anderson, *The Future of the Self: Inventing the Postmodern Person*. NY Tarcher/Putnam, 1999. Anderson, a social philosopher, argues that the idea of a single brain-centred self is no longer relevant in modern life and that each of us has a composite self put together from many factors. This is to be

expected in the post-Christian West, when there is no common narrative.

2. The palaeontologist Ian Tattersall describes the appearance of the Cro-Magnons as a kind of Big Bang when clearly self-conscious humans appeared. See his *Becoming Human: Evolution and Human Uniqueness*. OUP, 1998. Using the same metaphor, the appearance of entheistic man may be regarded as a second explosion.

3. Julian Jaynes, *The Origins of Consciousness in the Breakdown of the Bicameral Mind*. Boston: Houghton Mifflin, 1976. p. 149. Penguin reprint 1993.

4. Quoted in Al Gore, *The Assault on Reason*. London: Bloomsbury, 2008. p. 94.

5. The recently invented term "fake news" does not do justice to the pervasiveness of this hidden propaganda. One very worrying aspect is that the impartiality of Wikipedia has been brought into question in the so-called "Philip Cross" case. The otherwise anonymous editor of that name has made some 30,000 controversial changes to *Wikipedia* entries, a figure which is clearly impossible for any one individual to achieve even if working all day and every day. One cannot escape the conclusion that there is a very substantial editorial group at work with broad instructions from the founder. Numerous requests for an answer to "Who is Philip Cross?" have drawn no response, other than to label the enquirers "conspiracy theorists", an all-purpose smear term that closes down dialogue and is intended to do so.

6. That the human self is in rapid transition, shaped by information technology is argued in many books. Typical is Sherry Turkle's *Life on the Screen: Identity in the Age of the Internet* (NY: Simon and Schuster, 1997) and *The Second Self: Computers and the Human Spirit* (NY:Basic Books, 2005. 3rd edn. 2017). Turkle sees the Internet as beneficial but problematic, enabling us to invent multiple selves online to suit the occasion, surely a perverse form of co-creation and risking mental illness.

7. Ernest Hilgard, *Divided Consciousness: Human Thought and Action*. Hoboken NJ: John Wiley and Sons, 1977. Expanded edn., 1986.

8. Ernest Hilgard, *Dissociation and Theories of Hypnosis*, Hoboken NJ: John Wiley and Sons, 1992: p. 77].

9. See, e.g., Paul MacLean, "The Triune Brain, Emotions and Scientific Bias" in F. G. Schmidt, ed. *The Neurosciences: Second Study*

Program. NY: Rockefeller University Press, 1990. pp. 336-349. A short and simplified version of the theory is available as a PDF, "The Triune Brain" (1999).

10. The diagram represents a vertical cross section of the brain only and should be complemented by a horizontal section, showing the vital function of the double brain, commonly referred to as the male and female brain. This has been omitted here purely for reasons of space and to keep the book's evolutionary theme in focus.

11. J. Y. Lettvin, H. R. Maturana, W.S. McCullogh, W. H. Pitts, "What the frog's eye tells the frog's brain," *Proceedings of the International Review of Education*, Vol. 47, Issue ii, Nov. 1959. pp. 1940-1951. Available in PDF.

12. There is a surprising shortage of literature on the alien hand syndrome addressed to the lay reader. As usual, the *Wikipedia* article is a good introduction and overview.

CHAPTER 9
THE EVOLUTION OF GOD AND RELIGION

I pray that they may be one, as thou, Father, art in me and I in thee ... that they may be one, as we are one.

(John 17:21-23)

If I am to know God directly, I must be completely Him and He must become completely me, so this He and this I are one

Meister Eckhart

From gods to God

As our species has evolved, so too has its understanding of the entity, power or force to which we give the all-purpose label of God, the word now covering a wide array of meanings. Each human group has its own god, which it spells with a capital G and which plays a crucial role in defining the identity of the group. This generalisation held good until the French Revolution, when the idea of a secular - i.e., a god-free - state was legitimated and enforced. In an earlier period, when we were hunter-gatherers and primitive farmers it was reasonable for our forebears to think that this 'god' was manifested in the powers of nature, in the life-force that enabled things to grow and in thunder, lightning, wind and rain, which induced a sense of awe and of our littleness and helplessness. The French anthropologist Lucien Levy-Bruhl (1857-1939) labelled this phase of religious evolution *participation mystique*, a rather romantic term and somewhat misleading, insofar as it may suggest that our ancestors felt a fully conscious oneness with nature. This assumed state of participation could hardly be called religion, since it was not associated with any ritual or social structure, but was a dim and unfocused awareness. As such, it had the beneficial consequence that there were no religious wars in those times. Tribes did not fight each other over the same experienced reality and that surely is a future state of common religious consciousness for which the human race must aim.

Later these natural forces were objectified in different ways, marking the beginning of religion proper. First came totemism, when carved and painted representations of animals were used to represent various natural powers – the strength of the bear, the flight of the eagle, the swiftness of the deer, etc. The purpose of these totems was not clearly defined: they were not idols to be worshipped, but rather they expressed awareness of Nature, with a capital N, and a sense of mutual relationship with it. Then, as our ancestors moved to a pastoral and agricultural way of life, they personified the totem, turning it into an object of worship and a source of magical power, of which the golden calf in the Old Testament is a good example. Religion became largely a matter of pleading with these fabricated gods for various things, but mostly for increase in fertility. Hence they were often in the form of a bull or a pregnant woman. The delusion that one could in some way influence the imagined power within these artefacts, particularly by animal sacrifice, gave rise to a bargaining process that was at the heart of primitive religion. The reasoning behind it was that the hypothesized god would be more generous if one gave up something of great value. For this reason only the best, unblemished animals were reserved as gifts for the gods. Over many centuries the Israelites hauled themselves out of idol worship, and the scorn that the prophets poured on the gods of their less enlightened neighbours is well expressed in a passage from Psalm 135:15-18 "They have mouths but cannot speak, eyes that cannot see, ears that cannot hear. There is no breath in their nostrils, and their makers and those who trust in them grow like them." It is understandable then that the Israelites, who forbade the making and use of idols, felt themselves as exceptional. They had every right to consider themselves a chosen people in this important respect.

The theology of appeasement and bribery was taken to an extreme in the practice of child-sacrifice, which was a particular feature of the culture of the Canaanites and particularly of the Phoenicians, who spread it across the Mediterranean. Archaeological excavations at Carthage have revealed the graves of several thousand children who were deliberately killed to appease the god Moloch. At one period child-sacrifice was practised by the Jews, the centre for this ritual, Tophet, actually being just outside Jerusalem. The Old Testament records its official ending in a roundabout way, with the story of how Yahweh, having ordered Abraham to sacrifice his son, then changed his mind and told him to sacrifice a ram instead (*Genesis* 22:1-19). The legend is a coded account of the abandonment of this grisly practice, but the fact that the story had to be invented and become part of the Jews' sacred scripture indicates that at one time there must have been a sizeable number of Jews who favoured child sacrifice. Their reasoning would have been that giving to this imagined god something so valuable as their own children would surely be the most powerful way to influence it. Doubtless there were traditionalists who objected strongly when the practice was ended and forbidden, arguing that this was the faith of their fathers. The most obvious objectors would have been the priests whose identity and social status depended on the old way of doing things. Similar resistance can be expected in any circumstances when radical change to a religion is proposed, not least when the self-sacrifice of Jesus to his heavenly father is brought into question.

What is of particular interest is that the bargaining attitude of mind which lies behind sacrificial religion persists to this day in both Judaism and Christianity. The Law, which Jesus in the gospels both defends and criticises, is at base a refined version of this contractual mentality, for the God of the Jews delivers reliably but only in proportion to the extent that his moral laws are kept. Christianity is a sacrificial religion in a somewhat different way, as an atonement, with Jesus offering himself to his father in heaven as a comprehensive blood offering for the sins of humankind, for the sin of Adam and my sins personally. How could a father in heaven not be moved by such generosity of spirit? This is the cruel and cockeyed logic that underlies the Christian narrative and it cuts totally across the message of God as a loving father in heaven, which Jesus preached so movingly in the parable of the Prodigal Son. There is a clear need today to escape from the self-contradictory God of traditional Christianity and a first step must be the removal of the stone altar which is the focus of Catholic and other places of worship. Were this to be proposed officially, one wonders how many priests would feel a loss of identity and argue for keeping the old ways.

A different way in which the powers of nature were divinised and became part of religion was through the invention of mythical personalities in a mythical other world; in the case of the Greeks, on top of Mount Olympus and Valhalla in the case of the Scandinavian gods. We see different analogues of the "same storm and fertility" gods across Norse, Greek, Roman and Hindu cultures and it is particularly interesting that Yahweh, the god of Jesus, originated as a Semitic storm god exactly in parallel with the Norse god Thor, who is still unconsciously honoured in the English word *Thursday*, meaning originally Thor's day. Yahweh, it should be said, was the god of the nomadic Kenite tribe into which Moses apparently married and seems then to have been folded into Hebrew theology. More to the present point is that Paul, preaching mostly to Greeks, and himself educated in a Graeco-Roman culture, slipped naturally into preaching the *Christos* in Greek mythological terms that they would understand, representing him as a flesh and blood demigod come down from above, just as Greek gods and goddesses moved effortlessly between earth and their natural abode above the earth.

This is a highly compressed and simplified account of the way in which man's understanding of the reality to which we give the name

"God" has changed over the centuries. Religion has evolved as our understanding of this creative power has evolved and there is no reason to think that it has stopped evolving. Indeed, there is every reason to think that we stand on the threshold of an epoch-making change. Before going into that it should be said also that major religions, once founded, evolve in two main ways. Firstly, they grow by small changes, often by borrowing elements from other religions. In Judaism, for instance, and later in Christianity Satan, the fallen angel, the tempter and arch-enemy of God, was taken from the Zoroastrian religion of the Persians. Secondly, as in science, periods of slow growth are punctuated by radical upheavals and a re-laying of foundations to which the philosopher Thomas Kuhn gave the term "paradigm change". At such times unquestionable assumptions are brought under examination and this gives rise to a period of emotionally charged debate, after which a core element of the old belief structure is rejected, replaced and what is effectively a new religion comes into existence. Sometimes the original dies, sometimes it lives on in parallel with the new. The underlying thrust of the present work is that just as Christianity can be seen as emerging through a paradigm shift in Judaism, when the concept of the Law and the exclusivity of the Jews was abandoned, a new religion is struggling now to be born from a new understanding of God, a religion in which the mythological narrative of Christianity is abandoned. From this post-Christian theology emerges a new and dynamic understanding of incarnation, prayer and ascesis. The Trinitarian God of Christianity has been the most powerful driving force of Western civilisation, and the profound emotional upheaval that will follow from making such great changes cannot be underestimated. In Luke's gospel (12:53) Jesus says that his message will "set a man against his father and a daughter against her mother", but there is every reason think that Luke is not quoting Jesus but actually referring to the disruptive impact of Pauline Christianity on the Jewish community, to which Jesus was totally committed, and it would be naive to think that credal Christianity will undergo a similar paradigm shift without the same most painful kind of antagonisms being aroused. All that one can do in such a situation is to keep in mind Augustine's words, "in all things charity".

From theism to entheism

Religions are usually classified by words that signal various interpretations of the Latin and Greek words for "god", *deus* and *theos*.
Atheism is, of course, belief that no such entity exists.

Deism assumes that there is a creating power of some kind but that it is completely unknowable and we have no communication with it, nor it with us.

Theism usually attributes personality to this god, believes that we can be in touch with it and are under a moral imperative to follow its laws. Theists hold that this god is quite separate from us and many Christian authorities (notably, Calvin in the past and Karl Barth more recently) insist that we must emphasize this separateness in order to avoid delusionary pride. However, other theologians, as quoted in the present work, emphasize the interconnecting role of the Holy Spirit, the "go-between God" and "that of God in all men". Thus Christianity is a theistic religion, but with a critical ambiguity, a God who is "out there" but in some obscure fashion "within" humans.

Polytheism is belief in many gods, sometimes ranked in order of importance, from household gods which were guardians of the family to high gods which protected the state and usually a single all-powerful god which created the world and made things happen on a global level.

Monotheism is belief in a single creating power.

Pantheism assumes that god is present and diffused in all things, particularly in nature. It is implicitly rejected by Christianity, since the early church saw pantheism in opposition to God-in-Christ and suspiciously close to the fertility rites of the heathens from which its parent Judaism had escaped.

Panentheism is a term invented by the German philosopher Karl Krause (1781-1832) to bridge the gap between pantheism and Christian theology. Panentheists broadly accept the premises of pantheism but hold that while divinity is in everything, it is present in a particular and significant way within the human species.

Entheism is a term first appearing in the theory of religion of the German poet and philosopher Novalis (1772-1801), who considered it a form of religion that was both revolutionary and experiential. It is, in his words, "The theory of the future of humanity .... Every human being who now lives from God and through God should himself become God [1]." After Novalis, the term entheism dropped out of use but has recently been adopted, mostly on the Internet, to cover theologies of a vaguely panentheistic and ethical nature, one website, for instance, defining its purpose as to "encourage the free and open construction of new systems of existential meaning which complement human rights and our symbiosis with the earth." As against this vagueness, the term is used in the present work with sharp definition, which will be explained and developed in the following chapter. It shares with Novalis the broad sense of God in creation and the centrality of experiential religion but will extend it in two critical ways, so that it should not be confused with what he, and others, understood by the term. Entheism, as the term is introduced, or re-introduced, here, takes as axiomatic that *Homo sapiens* is an evolved and evolving species and that cosmological science is opening up a vista of an evolving universe. These two facts were both unknown 200 years ago and, when pursued, lead ultimately to a new understanding of religion and science.

Notes and References
1. Quoted in Benjamin D. Crowe, "On the Religion of the Visible Universe: Novalis and the Pantheism Convroversy," *British Journal for the History of Philosophy*, 16 (1) 2008, p. 133.

CHAPTER 10
ENTHEISM AND THE FUTURE OF RELIGION

> *I am being driven forward*
> *Into an unknown land.*
> *The path grows steeper,*
> *The air is cooler and sharper.*
> *A wind from my unknown goal*
> *Stirs the strings of expectation.*
>
> Dag Hammarskjold, Secretary General of the UN, 1953-61 [1]

An outline of Entheism

As used henceforth, entheism will refer to a religious system based on the following beliefs:

- that there is a primal creating force which is the ultimate source of human consciousness
- that humans at a certain level of evolutionary development can be in two-way communication with it
- that the meaning and purpose of life is to identify one's core self and align one's behaviour with the hypothesized purpose of this creating source.

From this system emerge practical consequences of various kinds, notably behavioural change and the coming together of groups of "entheists" for mutual support, education and to propagate the new consciousness. An entheistic community must of its nature be both inward and outward looking, assisting members in the primary activity of "knowing God" and at the same time enabling the "new good news" to be communicated to those who may feel a need to have God in their lives. It goes without saying that initially those who feel this need will have little or no idea of the form that fulfilment will ultimately take.

It will immediately be seen that these three acts of faith are a restatement in somewhat more formal language of what Jesus and Paul taught about our relationship to God, as indeed did many individuals from other religious cultures. Stripped of cultural forms of expression, the substance of entheism can be recognized in the Hindu doctrine of *advaita* and in Islamic Sufism. It can be found also in Socrates and in Stoicism, particularly in Epictetus (50-135), who places great emphasis on trust in God, though he calls this God Zeus, rather than

Yahweh, as is to be expected. The following two passages from Epictetus could have been taken without change from Eckhart, apart from the ambiguous phrase "become a God", which calls for tighter definition of what being Godlike means. There is a striking echo in the second of Jesus' response to his disciples' request about how to pray, "Go into your room and shut the door and pray to your Father, who is in secret" (Matt 6:5-6).

> *Who then is a Stoic? Show me a man desiring to be of one mind with God, allowing nothing to disappoint, to cross him, to yield neither to anger, envy nor jealousy - in a word a man that would fain become a God, one that while still imprisoned in this dead body makes fellowship with God his aim.* [2]

and

> *When you close your doors and make it dark inside. Remember never to say you are alone, because you are not. God is inside and your own divine spirit too .... It is to this God that you should swear allegiance, as soldiers do to Caesar.* [3]

Every culture has its own creation story and Graeco-Roman philosophers of the Socratic tradition agree with those of the Judaeo-Christian tradition in holding that God created man in his own image and likeness. What is of particular interest, however, is how they differ in identifying this likeness. The Greeks regarded human intelligence not only as a gift from God but as the divine element within us. This is the *Logos*, which Epictetus refers to as the *logike dynamis* (*Discourses*, 1.1.4), that is, the reasoning power in humans that he identifies with the *Daimon* or divine spirit within. By contrast, the Jewish emphasis on the divine within is an ethical insight. The serpent in the first chapter of *Genesis* makes this point when it tells Adam and Eve that if they eat of "the fruit of the tree of knowledge of good and evil," they will "become as Gods". The Greek emphasis on intellect, as a critical aspect of "that of God within", has been challenged by many Christian authorities and is summed up in the often quoted phrase of Tertullian (155-240), "What has Jerusalem to do with Athens?", which is frequently used as an excuse for Christian anti-intellectualism. Entheism represents a natural fusing of intellect and spiritual intuition and thus it offers in principle a new challenge and new reward to the spiritual seeker. It can be seen as the converging of two great historical streams of intellectual and ethical evolution, both together holding the promise of something greater than each separately.

Insofar as any individual may be in agreement with the three acts of faith just noted and self-consciously within the flow of evolution, he or she may be identified with Paul's *kainos anthropos*, the new human, which translates literally into the Latin *Homo novus*. *Homo novus* may be taken as the scientific term for the hypothesized next developmental state of the species. Thus *entheism* may be considered as co-extensive with *novalism* (but only accidentally related to Novalis), which is taken to be both the habitual conscious state of *Homo novus* and the belief system summarized above. Both terms, entheism and novalism, refer to the same phenomenon but entheism approaches it as a dynamic new kind of spirituality, whereas novalism approaches it as an aspect of anthropology. As time goes by, it is to be expected that the two terms will become closer and complementary. Sadly, many sincere and spiritually sensitive Christians will experience entheism as an existential threat. A reflex of rejection can hardly be avoided by those who see Jesus of Nazareth as an object of worship or as the only son of God, self-sacrificed for our sins.

The terms *entheism* and *novalism* can be little more than word-play until there are in existence principles and praxis to take us systematically to a level of human consciousness where oneness with the creating power is seen and experienced as a natural and habitual state. It is a hunger for this experience of oneness that gives impetus to entheism. If its theo-logic is right, entheism must deliver what other religions do not even offer. It will have no appeal for those whose need is for a God to whom one goes now and then to obtain various desirables in life, much as one keeps a cow for milk, as Eckhart strikingly put it. There are also many today who feel a vague but nagging need for some kind of spiritual satisfaction but nothing so radical as entheism implies. Not infrequently the language used in expressing this lesser need tends to treat spirituality as if it was a new acquisition, a talent or personal enhancement, like learning to paint or getting a sun tan. Self-transformation is rarely, if ever, mentioned and almost never the fact that in order to gain it something will have to be given up with a long and difficult struggle.

The sense of oneness with the divine that is the fruit of spirituality comes only after giving up what seems to us the most precious thing of all, our familiar self-identity. This will be almost impossible in socially undeveloped and illiterate societies, where women are suppressed and devalued and there is no tradition of independent enquiry of any kind. The new theology will also find little welcome in cultures which may be technically advanced but which emphasize conformity and obedience to authority. This is often a legacy of Confucianism and Taoism, which put a high value on social stability. In such situations self-value is closely bound to social usefulness, and hence to preach that the "natural" self must, in the words of Jesus, die as a grain of wheat falls into the earth and dies if it is to become fruitful (*John* 12:24) will fall largely on deaf ears. The first task in such situations is, paradoxically, to build up ego-strength. Only then will the individual have a self to surrender. It is worth noting that neither the Creed nor the Lord's Prayer contain a hint that releasing our spiritual potential will call for such a wrenching decision or the long drawn out process of transformation that must then follow, and this strongly suggests that they are fitted only for the first stage of the spiritual journey.

Entheism as cognition

Rudolf Otto described God, the primal reality, as *mysterium tremendum et fascinans*, but the fact that we humans can know God at all is almost as tremendous a mystery, considering that our species is a branch of the ape family and each of us retains a vestigial tail, the coccyx, at the base of our spine as a reminder. The universe is about fourteen billion years old, so far as we can calculate, and we have gone in an evolutionary blink from swinging in the trees and communicating in grunts to putting members of our species on the moon. If a visitor from Mars, surveying our ancestors fifty thousand years ago, had been told that this would happen, he (or she?) would have tapped his head. As regards our future, anyone who hypothesises that having an habitual sense of God will be the next step in human evolution and an advance beyond traditional Christianity may expect to be greeted with the same disbelief. There will be a knee-jerk rejection firstly by scientists, since biologists and anthropologists will find nothing in our past to justify such a notion, secondly, by most religionists, since it would make much of existing belief systems obsolete, and, thirdly, by the uncommitted lay person, since it is hard to imagine or even understand what such a radical self-transformation would be or what it would require. Certainly, very few would accept it if it were on offer. Barring a gifted and far-sighted few, we do not know what it is like to feel ourselves as co-creators or identify our deepest self with the creating power which is our historical source. Nevertheless, the argument here being put forward is that the future of our species lies in the hands of those who feel called to this new kind of knowing and the behavioural change that it will necessarily demand.

The word *entheism* covers a doctrine, a state of consciousness or a way of life. Entheistic awareness can be seen as a composite of several kinds of consciousness which blend into an habitual and subliminal conscious state, essentially a pervading sense of the reality and omnipresence of an unseen power and of one's essential connection with it. Seen as a meditative state in which all thinking and imagination ceases in a state of "unknowing", entheism is close to the *via negativa* of many spiritual teachers, which emphasizes the necessity of abandoning words or mental images to prepare the mind for the experience of oneness. The entheistic approach, as will later be proposed, differs only in suggesting a more reliable method of entering into the state of oneness than that which is offered by other methods, such as centring prayer, mindfulness, mantra meditation or breath control. The sense of oneness which blots out all other mental activity during the time of meditation may happen half-planned in meditation after something like a "gestalt switch", and sometimes unexpectedly, when one is, as it were, invaded by a new awareness, as recorded by the hundreds of ordinary people who contributed to Alister Hardy's anthology of such experiences. All the great teachers of mystical theology are in agreement that rapturous manifestations, when the mystic gets "blissed out" are incidental and irrelevant, but unfortunately there is a common misunderstanding that they are the experience itself. Religious artists of the past were at a loss to represent the experience of oneness and the profound tranquility which accompanies it and have spread this misunderstanding. One famous example is Bernini's statue of Teresa of Avila in Rome, which shows her in something akin to an orgasmic swoon, and a photo of which adorns the cover of one edition of Evelyn Underhill's now classic work *Mysticism*. The reality is that the time of meditation is more often than not a matter of waiting with what the author of *The Cloud of Unknowing* calls "naked intent". Initially nothing much happens except frustration as one's mind is bombarded with mental chatter and distractions of all kinds. Later the dedicated waiting results in what Eckhart describes as a breakthrough (*durchbrechen*), dissolving or melting (*schmelzen*). Above all it is a sense of the rightness and unity of things and of being loved by an invisible and intangible reality. In this respect a sentence given in a vision to the mystic Julian of Norwich (1342-1416) is often quoted, "All will be well and all will be well, and every kind of thing will be well." This is not just pollyanna piety, for she had suffered greatly from deep awareness of the evil in the world and had been within inches of death in some undiagnosed disease. Initially entheism must contain a large component of blind faith in the existence of the reality with which one seeks communication, after which comes deliberate and self-conscious trust, until trust eventually develops into the sort of taken-for-granted certainty and security that Jesus preached when he said that one must become as a little child to enter the kingdom of God (Matt 18:3-4). It is by no means stretching the sense of his words to equate entering the kingdom with acquiring entheistic consciousness. The child does not worry about the future or the past but simply assumes that its parents will take care of things and such lack of apprehension is in the nature of entheism as it is in the nature of childhood.

Set against normal human consciousness, this new God-awareness is something like an extra sense, added to Aristotle's normal five or the modern psychologists' eight or nine. It is also a kind of feeling insofar as it is unanalysed of its nature. As a permanent state, as against occasional exalted moments, it might be compared to the kind of subliminal awareness of the bus driver, who, when turning a corner, knows where the rear end of the bus is and makes allowance for it, though not normally by concentrating on it. In a similar way, the God-aware individual behaves and perceives in a "Godly" way, while not thinking particularly about God. Apart from when it issues in meditational states, God-awareness is normally in the background, changing in intensity, rising or falling as our attention is focused on some normal daily activity. Those activities which call for concentration make simultaneous God-awareness impossible, but this is to oversimplify and there is much more to be said about mindfulness and what de Caussade called "the sacrament of the present moment". Awareness of the divine behind all appearances can come unexpectedly, for example when our attention is seized (the word is very appropriate) by the beauty of a flower, a mountain view, a particularly moving piece of music or many other such things. For most of our waking day, however, such awareness remains unstimulated. As Wordsworth says in his poem *Peter Bell*, "A primrose by a river's brim a yellow primrose was to him and it was nothing more." Religion in general knows this constant revelation of God in his creation mostly as something given to the exceptional individuals whom we call saints. For the "new human", although it is experienced in different degrees, God-awareness should be taken as normal.

Unitary consciousness, where conventional self and God-self fuse, is found in Hindu theology as *advaita*, or not two-ness and is often expressed in the Sanskrit phrase *Tat tuam asi*, translated as "Thou art that", and signifying that wherever one looks in nature God is to be found. Entheistic consciousness would differ from this slightly, but critically, in reversing the word order in English to "That Thou art", thus emphasizing simple recognition of the existence of the power we call God and affirming its reality. "That Thou art" thus becomes a sort of three word creed which is at the same time an act of recognition and of worship. Growth in spirituality, and thus growth in humanity, consists essentially in the increasing frequency and depth of such moments of recognition until they blend into continuity. The resultant state is an enlightenment but paradoxically a darkness, confirmed by most of the great mystical writers and summarised in the title of the influential but anonymous mediaeval work *The Cloud of Unknowing*. The darkness is paradoxical and not much emphasized by spiritual writers, perhaps for that reason. The expression "dark night of the soul" has come into the language since its first use by St John of the Cross, who is generally regarded as the most reliable guide in matters of mystical religion. In this instance, however, he does not distinguish very clearly between the sense of disorientation that follows from closing down our normal ways of knowing and what is usually called "dryness", when the sense of God disappears and one must continue the search for God without any obvious reason. Most of the reliable guides in this darkness are to be found in the pages of past masters of the spiritual life, and they do not speak with one voice. The darkness of entheism can be a positive experience, when one has learned to give up all attempts to understand in a human way and, against the reflex attempts of our natural curiosity, rest in a kind of blankness. Eckhart calls it "knowing by not knowing" and "living without a why". It can be a dark night when one is aware of failure to attain to that state and feelings of frustration and failure arise, but the condition is treatable with the all-purpose remedy of trust.

"Knowing God" is by no means a transparent phrase, for it calls for abandonment of normal ways of knowing. We have to disable these in order to experience what is, in one important sense, an empathic knowing. This is the kind of knowledge that lovers experience and in the present instant calls for a disabling of the mind, which seeks naturally to categorize, theorize and draw logical conclusions. All of these are worse than useless, for they distract us from the effort required to meet God in the silence. Eckhart emphasizes this fact and attempts to achieve the necessary disablement of normal thought processes by leaving us with a series of paradoxes, and in this his teaching has been compared with the methods of Zen Buddhism [4]. He is acutely aware that spiritual knowledge is quite different from all other kinds, which he lumps together as "lower". In knowing God we are, in his words, detached from "all objective bodily things and in a state where we hear without sound and see without matter, where there is neither white nor black nor red." What is almost humorously paradoxical is that all this teaching of mindlessness and knowing by not knowing rests upon the basis of a theological subtlety that he puts forward in distinguishing between God and the Deity (or Godhead). This in turn rests, as already noted, on an epistemological distinction between reality in itself and the limited aspect of reality which is accessible to our limited human understanding. Once that is understood, it is easy to appreciate that we were not created originally out of "nothing" but out of the Deity itself and that in turn drives us to return our individual self to its origin, to re-establish a primal unity. The mystery will always remain, but at least we become more aware of its existence.

God in nature

Learning to see and feel God in nature provides an entry into a more constant and deeper kind of cognition and comes simply from giving deliberate attention to the beauty around us, for this is sufficient to induce awareness of what Wordsworth called "something far more deeply interfused." Experiencing God in nature is of course nothing new in theology. It appears in the psalms in phrases such as "the heavens show forth the glory of the Lord", but, perhaps surprisingly, only briefly and obliquely in the New Testament. In fact, the only mention that comes to mind is Jesus's injunction to "consider the lilies of the field" (Matt 6:25-34). The theological insight that God may be experienced in nature, or perhaps rather through nature, is very common in poetry, summarised in Elizabeth Barrett Browning's memorable line, "Earth's crammed with heaven and every common bush afire with God", but, as she notes immediately, only for those who see. Her brief qualification is probably more important than it may at first seem, for each of us is born with a certain degree of sensitivity to the beauty of nature or to music, poetry or art - a kind of aesthetic or spirituality quotient, much as we have an intelligence quotient - and hence we are each blessed or limited in our ability to sense a higher beauty not only in nature but in human experience more generally. It is possible, for instance, to find God not only in the grandeur of nature but through a mental act in a multitude of everyday things and *through all our senses*, in the smile of a child, stroking the cat, a cold beer on a hot day or the wind on our face. We err in thinking that the direct experience of God is all mystical bliss and ecstasy, for this kind of bread-and-butter, non-verbal, non-religious mysticism is a genuine entry into communication with the divine. Once that is accepted, it becomes clear that how to develop this unsuspected method of prayer constitutes an important element in religious education.

Until quite recently it has always been marginal and optional in Christianity, often identified as Franciscan or Celtic spirituality, and somewhat suspect insofar as it can easily be confused with the secular religion of Gaia. Some modern prophets, however, have made it central in their teaching, among whom Thomas Berry and Brian Swimme hold a special place and the following quotation from the latter illustrates how close he came to what might be called the entheistic vision.

> *When you take the story of the universe as your basic referent, all your thoughts and actions are different. It is an awesome, wonder-full, uplifting, "Wow!" approach to human existence and our place in this universe. It is a different story about who we are, and its magnificence and grandeur have the capacity to call us into a new consciousness.* [5]

What science adds to traditional nature mysticism are the religious feelings that arise from contemplating the new universe that is being gifted to us by science, as ever more powerful telescopes reveal a universe of mind-numbing size and a wondrous machinery of galaxies, supernovae and black holes wheeling and interacting together. This vast expanding panorama is not nature as normally understood, but even the most hardened atheist can hardly contemplate it without experiencing a sense of awe. It should make us aware of our littleness, and indeed it does, but at the same time we can experience the most paradoxical feeling that it belongs to us. It is all ours and we experience, fleetingly or profoundly, the same feeling that Paul foreshadowed when he promised his early followers, "All is yours and you are Christ's and Christ is God's" (1 Cor 3:18-23).

This cosmic awareness is well expressed in the following two quotations, the first from Admiral Byrd's autobiographical work *Alone* in which he tells of going outside one evening as the sun was setting during his spell in Antarctica and of his experience:

> *of the imponderable processes and forces of the cosmos, harmonious and soundless ... In that instance I could feel no doubt of man's oneness with the universe. The conviction came that the rhythm was too orderly, too harmonious, too perfect to be a product of blind chance – that, therefore there must be purpose in the whole and that man was a part of the whole and not an accidental off-shoot, [that] the universe was a cosmos, not a chaos; man was as rightfully a part of that cosmos as were the day and night.* [6]

The second quotation is from the psychiatrist Richard Bucke's *Cosmic Consciousness*, a work of 1900, which is remarkable for its subtitle, *A Study in the Evolution of the Human Mind* and for the way in which he associates the feeling outlined by Byrd with moral and intellectual advancement and with a sense of oneness with the creating power. He describes it as

> *a consciousness of the cosmos, that is, of the life and order of the universe along with an intellectual enlightenment which alone would place the individual on a new plane of existence – would* **make him almost a member of a new species**. *To this is added a state of moral exaltation, an indescribable feeling of elevation, elation and joyousness, and a quickening of the moral sense, which is fully as striking.... With these come what may be called a sense of immortality, a consciousness of eternal life, not a conviction that he shall have this, but the consciousness that he has it already. (emphasis added)* [7]

Such transcendental experiences are by no means so rare as might be assumed and are a warrant of the pervading reality of a Power that is at once infinite – so far as we can understand the word – and at the same time deeply personal. Thanks to the initiative of the distinguished biologist Sir Alister Hardy (1896-1985) and his collaborators in setting up the Religious Experience Research Centre at the University of Wales; we now have an archive of thousands of accounts of similar experiences, usually in normal daily life, and almost all by individuals who would not consider themselves mystically inclined or even religious. Hardy's self-imposed task was to understand their significance by classifying them as a first step, and concluded that they are of such a variety that there are no "normal" patterns. The common factor is the sudden and unexpected sense of an external power along with heightened awareness, described typically by one correspondent as "a feeling of peace, a sort of light, a feeling of joy and warmth such as I have never ever before experienced" but which left a mental imprint in the form of "a strange sort of peace in periods of anxiety." Some respondents tell of what one describes as "a growing sense of personal encounter with a power at the same time within and outside me" and another as "a gradual unfolding of understanding, a slow development ... an immense drive I feel pushing me to deepen my knowledge of self [and] reach towards the whole meaning of the universe" [8]. Altogether, the many excerpts which Hardy selects provide a fascinating and puzzling phenomenon, but one is worth singling out here because it suggests an answer to that most urgent problem; "how is this seemingly random experience of God to be made available more systematically through religious practice"? The writer tells not of a sudden or dramatic event but how religion has become for her over a period of time "a less personal experience, more a sense of depth in and yet beyond myself" and how she "shared with others the Presence of God" in her Quaker group, adding, "A gathered Meeting is an awesome experience." I have noted in other writing that the gathered meeting is becoming something of a rarity in Quakerism today, and will return to this question below, when treating of the practical implications of entheism.

Notes and References

1. Dag Hammarskjold, *Markings*. London: Faber & Faber, 1964. p.31.
2. Quoted in Janet Baine Kopito (ed.), *The Philosophy of Epictetus: Golden Sayings and Fragments*. Mineola, NY: Dover Publications, 2017. p. 30.
3. Epictetus, *Discourses, 1:14*. Translated and quoted by A. A. Long, *Greek Models of Mind and Self*, Cambridge, MA: Harvard UP, 2015. p. 180.
4. Cyprian Smith, *The Way of Paradox*. London: Darton, Longman and Todd, 2004. p. 12. [1987]
5. Brian Swimme, *The Universe is a Green Dragon*. Santa Fe, NM: Bear and Co.1984. p. 58.
6. Richard Byrd, *Alone*, NY: Putnam, 1938. p. 38.
7. Richard M Bucke, *Cosmic Consciousness: A Study in the Evolution of the Human Mind*. NY: Carol Publishing Group, 1993 [1900]. p. 18.
8. Alister Hardy, *The Spiritual Nature of Man*. OUP, 1979. p. 70 and passim.

CHAPTER 11
THE NEW GOOD NEWS

Contemplation is the only ultimate answer to the unreal and insane world that our financial systems and our advertising culture and our chaotic and unexamined emotions encourage us to inhabit. To learn contemplative practice is to learn what we need so as to live truthfully and honestly and lovingly. It is a deeply revolutionary matter.

Archbishop Rowan Williams [1]

The new God-story

The English word *gospel* and the Greek word *evangelion* both have their roots in the meaning "good news", but they only tell us half of it. The other half we may find today in the various branches of science which are revealing marvellous things about the created universe and about human nature. An indication of this has already been given in the emergence of neurotheology but there is much more to come, especially in cosmotheology. Esoteric as this may at first appear, most of it is capable of being presented quite simply in story form that can enthral an eight year old. That is a task awaiting those gifted story-tellers who know intuitively how children feel and understand. Such authors can turn their gifts into cash today (the writer of the Harry Potter books is reputedly worth half a billion pounds) but the challenge here has a greater prize in store, nothing less than helping to create the global family envisioned by St Paul, in which there would be "neither Jew nor gentile, slave or free, male or female". The new humans would be bound by a historical and futuristic narrative that transcends all the tribal mythologies of the past and by a common experience of the divine creating power. If the creation story of science is presented in the right way, the wonder of it will cross cultural boundaries, though it will have to co-exist for a long time with existing myths and legends until, without need for crusade or jihad, it comes to be the commonly accepted framework for understanding what it means to be fully human.

The day when this comes about may be far into the future, but the vision is here now and ready to be actualised in many places on a small scale. As these new and experimental communities multiply, we shall have that seemingly impossible ideal, a true global family with a shared understanding of God overriding the tribal identities which have been the norm since humans first appeared. This ever divisive and seemingly "natural" tribalism has generated endless wars, untold misery and a planet which is now self-destructing. A global community will create its identity from the freshly minted story of our cosmic and evolutionary origins, of the great men and women from many countries and many cultures and the heroic deeds of discovery, endurance and self-sacrifice which have taken our species upward step by step to new levels of humanisation. The phrases "global community" or "global family" will be meaningless to many well-intentioned people, and the theological work now facing us will be to make it meaningful and create the structures, physical, educational and economic that will be required. The spiritual quest now is for an intimate and cooperative relationship. We must go forward very tentatively here, in the dark, often by touch, experimentally but acting decisively when clarity is given. There is so much to learn, but most of all we need to know more about how to take the steps into the silence, when the ineffable experience of a higher, loving power just happens and everything in our world changes.

The new global narrative may have its roots in science but will demand no more mathematics than one wishes to bring to it, and it can be fitted to the needs and capacity of anyone with natural curiosity, from the brainiest adult to the child in primary school. The essence of the story can be compressed into the following graphic representation.

Figure 6 From the Big Bang to man the co-creator

All this is proposed before there is any programme or structure in existence, but at some future time a learning programme will emerge that will help create the new consciousness through all modes of intellectual and artistic experience. We in the West live today with the shreds of a bygone culture, surrounded by the triviality, incoherence and coarseness of much modern art, poetry, music and architecture alongside the nostalgic relics of a bygone "age of faith". We cannot go back; a new source of inspiration is our only hope, and it lies there like a book waiting to be opened. Cosmic and human evolution is now telling a 'wonder-full' and 'meaning-full' story, but it needs to be translated to show God at work in the world, in nature and in our mind and feelings. As it is propagated and pervades common consciousness we may hope to see it eventually embodied in architecture and design as inspiring as the mediaeval cathedrals, the exuberant temple ornament of Hinduism and the austere symmetrical art of the mosque, in new epic narratives, new art and music that tells the story, as inspired as once were the Bach Passions and Handel's *Messiah*.

All comes together slowly to create a new kind of knowing and feeling, and it is worth noting how Paul describes the hypothesized end point of this process in the intriguing phrase, "Then shall I know as I am known" (I Cor 13:12), thus implying that "knowing God" is a reciprocal action but also that the initiative does not come from the human side of the partnership. Our role is simply not to say no when the impulse is felt. Partnership is perhaps not quite the right word, and one suspects that Eckhart would argue that we err in thinking that there are two participants in a dialogue, for in calling God "the spark of the soul", which he often does, he suggests audaciously that the divine-human relationship is not so much God and man in conversation as God almighty in dialogue with God incarnated in each of us. Eckhart puts it in a nutshell when he says,

> *God expects but one thing from you that you let God be God in you.*

Here we can see the beginnings of a dramatically new doctrine of incarnation and co-creation. The new story will be very different from the traditional story of the Old and New Testaments. It will be, in fact, not so much a narrative as a drama in which we are all players.

Entheism as co-creation

Teresa of Avila said that God has no hands but ours, but Eckhart goes much further in implying a more pro-active attitude towards human evolution. To postulate a divine timeless consciousness, actualised in time as human consciousness, confronts religion with a huge challenge, for it changes the assumed purpose of religion from passive obedience to a distant creator to an habitual sense of cooperating with it, an attitude which shades into union at some deep level of awareness. The model of a loving heavenly father which Jesus sought to overlay on primitive Yahwism can thus be seen as appropriate only to the first stage of spiritual development, well fitted to an earlier and theologically naïve era and still perhaps largely fitted as an introduction to Jesus for illiterate communities and for children today before they move on to an adult understanding. But if that strategy be adopted as appropriate in any particular situation, a way must be found to abandon the doctrine of a supposedly loving father-god who set up his only son's agonizing death as a satisfying atonement for humanity's sins. To refocus religion on developing an attitude of active cooperation rather than humble worship may at first seem to be taking an unprecedented liberty, but in fact is an attitude that can only be adopted with a deep sense of dependence and trust.

How realistic?

In bringing logical heads and intuitive hearts into a harmony entheism creates a new kind of consciousness from their mutual resonance, and as this intensifies within the group, religion cannot but take on a new vitality, change our lives, make us happy and capable of making others happy, and fill us with love that comes from the knowledge that we are an integral part of the Great Reality. Difficulty should not be confused with impossibility nor should the evolutionary vision be abandoned because it cannot be implemented within our lifetime. Spiritual explorers must take the long-term view, do their bit, put their brick in the wall and leave the unfinished edifice to the future. One may take heart from looking back in history and seeing how human nature has changed, but aware of the length of time that change has taken. Our forebears, for example, might never have started on the long road to the abolition of slavery if they had considered how impossible it was by human standards. Chattel slavery was accepted as part of the natural order for thousands of years, actively defended by great thinkers such as Aristotle and passively accepted by virtually all. Jesus himself seems not to have thought it important enough to mention, so far as we can tell from the gospels. A Gallup poll at that time would probably have shown a very small fraction of one per cent of the free population in favour of a slave-free society or would even accept it as an ideal. The institution of slavery was in effect a near-universal moral blind spot, few could imagine a society without it; nobody spoke out against it in ancient times and very few closer to our own times. Two hundred years ago the Church of England in Barbados branded its plantation slaves as proof of ownership [2] and even so great a spiritual and social reformer as William Penn owned slaves and bequeathed them in his will as a possession, as did George Washington and several of the Founding Fathers of America, the "land of the free". Although Quakers led the way in abolition, there are accounts of early preachers in America being physically ejected from meeting houses for attempting to disturb the social order without any scriptural warrant. In a word, slavery was, with very few exceptions, accepted as normal and natural.

Most people could not imagine a slave-free society, as most people today could not imagine a society with a substantial proportion of noval humans, whose sense of self sprang from a profound identification with the power that created the universe. It took almost fifty years to go from the first political agitation to the abolition of slavery in the British Empire in 1833. Saudi Arabia fell into line with the rest of the world by abolishing it as late as 1963 and Mauritania finally in 1980. Looking back now, we can see that what happened was a fundamental shift in the world's sense of what it means to be human, but it took a long time and the work of many dedicated and mostly unknown campaigners who gave up their lives in order to bring it about. The moral numbness about slavery, only six or seven generations ago, should be set in the wider context of ethical evolution - that is, humanisation - for around the same time it was not considered morally repugnant to go for entertainment to public executions. The last public hanging in America was, in fact, held as recently as 1936 and attracted some 18,000 spectators. Against this background of slow but radical change in moral values, there is reason to expect that a change in spiritual perception, from a theistic to an entheistic and co-creative theology, may become apparent in the next century, at least in some parts of the world. It may seem impossible today and will be resisted by historically entrenched faiths, perhaps as strongly as was the abolition of slavery not so long ago. By the same token, however, there is reason to think that the new spirituality will overcome opposition in the long run.

We may take heart from reflecting on the strange and wonderful process in nature by which a caterpillar is totally transformed and becomes a butterfly, a transformation in which the caterpillar literally dies and is replaced by a new creature. The caterpillar, once hatched from the butterfly egg, eats voraciously, many times its own weight of vegetation each day, until it has expanded as far as its external skin will allow. At that point the skin hardens into a chrysalis within which the cellular structure of the caterpillar starts to break down. At the same time within the chrysalis tiny structures, which biologists call "imaginal cells", start to appear. (The term *imaginal* has nothing to do with *imaginary*, but refers to the technical Latin word *imago*, meaning the final shape of the developing organism.) At first these isolated imaginal cells are rejected by the caterpillar as foreign bodies and destroyed by its immune system. Eventually, however, they multiply to the point where the immune system cannot cope, fails entirely from stress and the invading cells multiply and start to join up in the latent shape of the butterfly to come. They feed on their host, the caterpillar, which by now has dissolved into cellular soup. After a week or two the butterfly is fully formed but tightly packed within the chrysalis, until one fine day the outer casing splits and the butterfly emerges and unfolds itself before flying off. What is most intriguing and germane to the present theme is that the caterpillar and the butterfly are two distinct creatures, each having its own genome, and how they got together remains a biological mystery [3].

This astonishing metamorphosis may be seen as an analogue of the way that moral and political transformation takes place in society. Awareness of the need for radical religious – and, indeed, evolutionary - change was for many centuries a dynamic that drove Christianity, but has been stalled since Christianity became the established religion in the West, to the point that it in some European countries it was supported by state taxation. In those early years Christians were conscious in varying degrees of being humans in process of transformation, although one should perhaps qualify that assertion by talking of "thinking or serious Christians". This awareness is seen vividly in the Book of Kells, an illustrated gospel from around 800 AD, with marginal and full page illustrations that are quite stunning in the wealth of love and spiritual insight that shines from its artistry and calligraphy. In the corner of one page of the brilliantly coloured text is a representation of metanoia in the form of the insect metamorphosis that has just been described in scientific terms. Two moths hold between them the chrysalis, which is destined to become a moth, as if they were supporting it through the process. A more powerful statement of the inner meaning of Christianity can hardly be imagined than this expression of Celtic spiritual genius. However, as Christianity has became the established religion, and its wonders taken for granted, the lively sense of Christian metanoia has diminished to the point of disappearance, resulting in the sort of crisis within religion about which Rahner, Bonhoeffer and many other spiritual writers write almost despairingly. If, however, we each see ourself as an imaginal cell working to build the butterfly of a better "me" and a better world in the future, a mental realignment will take place, quite suddenly. We will feel the need to link up with other like-minded individuals who have been converted to the same vision and seized by it and, at the same time, we will not be surprised or downcast when we are rejected by society's "immune system", for society cannot but resist such a shock to the status quo. Once linked up, three related problems come into view, namely, how to define the end goal for which we were created, how to present it to the world in an intelligible and achievable form and how to create structures designed to bring it about.

The real difficulty in religious paradigm change - and entheistic religion is nothing less - comes not from learning the new but unlearning the old. Should not, then, the primary task of a religion for our time be to build up this new spiritual consciousness over a long period using all the means that information technology now offers and all the wisdom and experience of the past, not least the mistakes? It is an unstated premise of the present work that the long term future of our planet depends on those who feel this logic in their bones, who know with certainty that they have unfulfilled potential which must now be unlocked and who sense their capacity for a new kind of consciousness that brings unshakeable happiness, no matter what life brings. We are at a crisis point, a critical fork, in human evolution, for it is becoming ever clearer that our technical skill has far outstripped both our intellectual and moral development. As a species we do not have the capacity to solve the problems we have created. We can make war in the most sophisticated way and pour economic resources into waging it, but we cannot make peace. We can give everyone a luxurious carriage that even princes could never have dreamed of a hundred years ago and a magic carpet of air travel that will whisk us half way across the globe in a few hours, but we cannot stop ourselves from destroying the planet's atmosphere, its forests and its seas [4]. We seem to be stuck at a level where our most primitive tribal reflexes have control over our brain, and we lack the vision and the logistical skills to develop our finest instincts and make them an active force for change.

As a goal for the species, rather than the spiritual calling for a few rare individuals, entheistic awareness would mark a defining evolutionary step to be ranked with the invention of fire or language. This is what Paul was trying to communicate, when he wrote that "Anyone who is in Christ is a new creature" (2 Cor 5:17). The actual change, however, is a process which every individual follows in his or her own way and at their own speed. Paul described the end point of this process of self-transformation in a memorable sentence, "Then shall I know as fully as I am known" (I Cor 13:12), thus implying that "knowing God" - which is entheism in a nutshell - emerges from the joint action of the divine and the human individual. We know by knowing that we are known! The human contribution may begin with active searching, wide reading and regular attendance at conferences and retreats, but it ends in a receptive waiting. Why any human should wish in the first place to embark upon on this journey into the transhuman is a question without an obvious answer. Many good people will not feel any such call. It is all very mysterious.

Notes and References

1. From an address given to the Synod of Catholic Bishops in Rome, Oct. 10, 2012.
2. The part played in abolition by the Church of England should also be noted, particularly by Wilberforce and Porteous, the Bishop of Chester. The full story is told in Adam Hochschild, *Bury the Chains*. London: Pan Reprints, 2012 (Macmillan, 2005). It is a sobering account of how inhuman humans can be and at the same time an inspiring story of how individuals, once seized by an ideal, can give up their lives to making it happen.
3. A short and non-technical account of how imaginal cells function to change the caterpillar into a butterfly can be found in Norrie Huddle, *Butterfly*. Self-published by Huddle Books, 1970, it has had a wide circulation and has been translated into Spanish with the title *La gran metamorfosis humana*.
4. The imminence and unsuspected extent of this threat is dealt with in my 2017 work, *The Global Energy Trap and a Way Out* (Leicester: Matador) but since then new data and violent weather events lead to an even more catastrophic prediction. Taken together with the massive and seemingly insoluble problem of the world's oceans polluted with plastic waste, the future of the planet looks very dim indeed.

CHAPTER 12
MAKING THE VISION A REALITY

We need a total revolution, not a financial or social or merely economic, outward revolution but, rather, a mutation, a complete change in the whole structure of consciousness.

J. Krishnamurti, *The Nature of the New Mind* [1]

The passage to entheism

As the fable of belling the cat tells us, there is not much point in having inspirational ideas unless there are the material and human resources required to make them happen. Without a practical plan to get from here to there, we shall end with nothing but fine thoughts. Since the goal of entheism is to attain a constant and deepening sense of oneness with our source, as Jesus and other evolutionary forerunners manifested, the first step must be to establish connection with this invisible and intangible reality as best we can. This is the purpose of meditation, but it is hedged with difficulties: what actually is religious or spiritual meditation, what methods are to be used, how will we recognize the experience of oneness, is divinity to be found in the silence or is it the silence itself, do we actively seek or wait to be grasped? The necessary starting point for all theistic meditation (but not, it should be emphasized, for Buddhist or transcendental meditation) is quite simple: we must ask the power which created us and of which we are an integral but minuscule part to reveal what needs to be done and put ourselves at its disposal. At first it is hardly possible to do this unselfconsciously, without wondering if we are talking to ourselves, so this first step is an act of belief that there is something or someone there who hears. The science of cosmic evolution now supports belief in a creating consciousness which is our source and of which each one of us is a kind of "time-bound atom of consciousness". Whatever new understanding of God and self may eventually emerge, it will need to co-exist for a long period with traditional concepts of God and thus for a while the spiritual seeker – on whom human evolution now depends – must live in two worlds, within the Christian narrative or other religious mythology while seeking to escape from it. In this situation the best advice is to delay a final decision until it seems to make itself [2]. Tugged between an unknown future and a past that we must leave behind, it is doubtless advisable to let the subconscious ultimately make the decision.

The theology of the future must be built on a foundation of knowledge of the past and all must engage in the common task of learning about the new creation story, seeing Jesus now not as a god disguised as a human being but as a unique guide and an elder brother with whom we are engaged in the common task of co-creation. This will without doubt be dismissed by orthodox Christians, almost as a reflex, as nothing more than the ancient heresy of Arianism in a new guise. Some may find it at first intellectually appealing and even exciting but will back off like the rich young man in Luke's gospel when a decision is called for, and this decision will surely challenge serious seekers to a painful call for giving-up long held beliefs. Every step into the new spiritual awareness demands a change in our familiar identity. Each stage of growth into the new will be a small death of the old, as new reflexes replace what previously were "natural" and automatic. Spiritual development must be at first awkward, somewhat like the normal person learning to write with the left hand. Especially in its early stage, this uncomfortable process can only be sustained by what might literally be called "dedicated hypocrisy": spiritual seekers must try to behave like someone they want to be but know that they are not yet there and not sure that they ever will be. Sometimes it will seem like a battle for one's very self, for that is exactly what it is.

We are all, as it were, addicted to the old "normal" self and the advice often given to the reforming alcoholic, "Fake it till you make it", is very applicable in this situation. "Act as if" is sound advice for those who seek to escape the addiction of the old familiar self and develop new behavioural reflexes. In every personal odyssey there must be a long stretch when the path of self-transformation will seem to be going against one's "real" nature, trying to act unselfishly while knowing how self-interested one can be, with patience when one is so easily irritated, without complaint when one's instinct (or so it seems) is to criticize and moan, with generosity when one knows how grabby and inconsiderate one can be. For almost all spiritual seekers, the journey to self-transformation begins with a very weak and intermittent experience of the kind of intimacy with God which Jesus talked about. Such intimacy, like a growing friendship, may take many years before it becomes habitual and "a new natural".

Without experiencing the tension of these almost schizoid feelings spiritual growth is hardly possible for most of us. Repeated failure is inevitable but it should not be taken as a reason to give up. In the first stages the spiritual seeker is rather like a five year old learning to write, with painful slowness and effort but unconsciously learning the fine motor control that will eventually result in a flowing and aesthetically pleasing script. Sometimes failure is so abject, especially perhaps when it comes to controlling our temper, over-indulging in food or sexual pleasure or slipping into backbiting gossip, that one may wonder if any progress has been made at all. In such circumstances it is easy to suspect that despite all the fine words, we are the same old incorrigible self. In all this, however, it must be remembered that the term "spiritual person", or even "mystic", does not mean someone who is a paragon of virtue but one who deliberately faces in a particular direction, whose self-will is increasingly and deliberately subordinated to a higher self and identified with it.

The entheistic group

Karl Rahner has been taken as an articulate example of many individuals who are seeking self-fulfilment in a more intimate relationship with God. What is missing from his analysis of the problem, and indeed from almost all writers on this theme, is awareness of two important consequences that follow from seeking this desired state. Firstly, to the extent that the goal is reached, it will have evolutionary significance, since the God-aware and God-centred individual is a different creature from the ordinary human being. When the spiritual and intellectual barriers to achieving this habitual state have been surmounted, one will have become not just a better, more virtuous human being but a new kind of human. It was for this reason that the contemporaries of Jesus felt intuitively that he was different in some fundamental way. Without any knowledge of human evolution, they could only explain this intuition by categorizing him as a latter day Elijah, the greatest of the prophets. A few years later, faced with the same problem, Christians decided that Jesus was different because he was the only son of the Jewish God, as the beautiful Apollo, the human ideal, was the son of the high god Zeus of the Greeks. Intriguingly, Jesus called himself "the son of man", a term which occurs 81 times in the gospels and continues to puzzle scholars. Used so often, it must surely be making an important statement about the way in which Jesus understood himself. It is by no means impossible that it was the gospel writers' way of putting into the mouth of Jesus something like "I am the representative new human", suggesting that he was an advance specimen, rather than a one-off.

The second missing element in a small flood of writing on the new spirituality is the awareness of the need for a new kind of religious group to serve those whom Rahner broadly refers to as mystics but here may be called entheists. A new kind of community must be called into being with which God-aware individuals can identify, within which they can grow, to which they can contribute and through which can propagate the "new good news". Theoretically such a novel community as is now required could grow within an existing organisation, acting as a leaven, and, if so, the new mysticism would be validated by the parent Church and discord could be avoided. This is uncannily like the situation in which Pauline Christianity found itself in its very early days, legitimised as an acceptably Jewish group at the First Council of Jerusalem in 48 AD (Acts 15:1-21). It was, however, an uneasy compromise and did not hold up for very long before the break came, as earlier noted, with Paul's Epistle to the Galatians, where the differences are made explicit in the strongest, even violent, terms. However, given that the quest for the direct experience of God which Rahner seeks is not an essential tenet of Christianity and is completely absent from the Christian creed, there is no reason to think that this exotic new doctrine of oneness would be welcomed as leaven by any established religion. It is more likely that its proponents would be regarded as a foreign body, as eventually were Paul's Jewish converts, and rejected as a foreign body, just as the physical body deals with infections. Nothing in history would suggest otherwise. It is worth noting at this point that in the Roman and some other branches of Christianity there have been for many centuries self-contained communities of so-called contemplatives, appropriately called "enclosed orders", but they have had little or no effect on mainstream Christian theology or practice. The normally religious person may admire and wonder at the saints but rarely feels called to imitate them.

The diagram represents the evolutionary path to Entheism. 'Decision 1' is a conscious choice to seek God. 'Decision 2' is a second choice to work towards trying to attain state 'of oneness with God'.

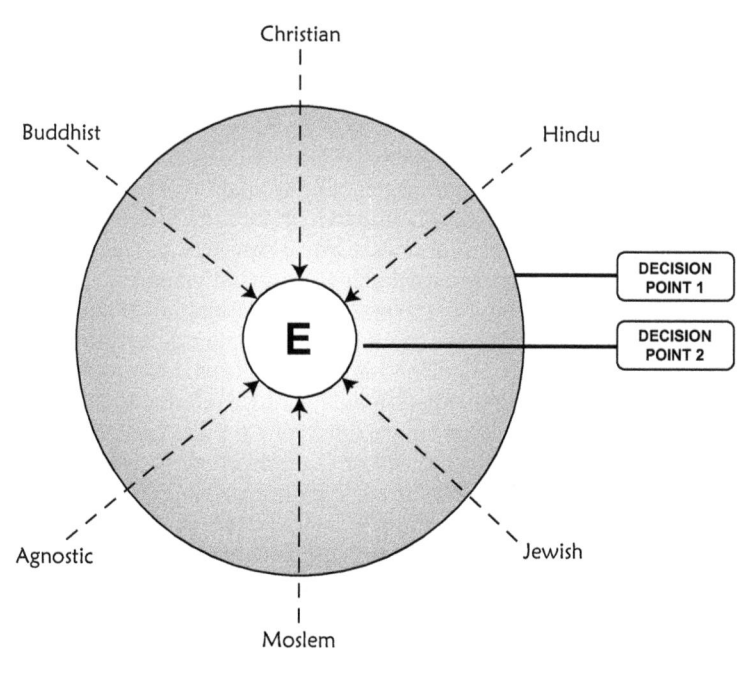

Figure 7 Hub and Spoke

Seen from this perspective, an evolutionary transition to entheism presents a knotty problem in church governance, indeed in organization theory. How might it be possible, even in theory, to create a dynamic movement dedicated to the new spirituality without fragmenting Christianity even further and generating yet more discord? The problem is made acute by the fact that many genuinely religious individuals simply do not understand what is at issue. The idea of oneness with God does not make sense for them except in the unique instance of Jesus and that an ordinary human can set out to attain it will seem not so much impossible as arrogant and delusional. In this context the experience of the Benedictine abbot John Chapman is of interest. He tells in his *Spiritual Letters* of an informal survey that he had carried out among a small number of monks and nuns to establish how many had experienced or had sought "the experience of oneness" and who practised wordless prayer with that end in view, since the two go together. He was somewhat disconcerted to find that that while some knew what he was talking about, the majority found his question hard to understand, among them some individuals whom he considered saintly [3]. This raises a profoundly important issue: is Christian spirituality possible without experiencing, or at least aiming for, the elusive sense of oneness with the divine that Jesus claimed for himself? Similar questions multiply. In what does this state of oneness differ from what might be called normal Christianity? What is the most effective way to pursue it? Is it a realistic goal for the ordinary man or woman? These questions must be addressed if religion is to move on into the future. Taking an evolutionary perspective throws a whole new light on the subject and opens a new debate. Are we looking here at individuals who have reached the peak of human development or is "Christian perfection" a significantly different state and a mark of *Homo novus*? Probably the best known commentator on the concept of religious perfection is John Wesley, who wrote about it at length. He referred to it as the "second blessing", religious conversion being the first, and marked by "complete surrender to the will of God". In effect he was asking the same question as Rahner: can ordinary humans know God in this mysteriously intimate way and, if so, why is normal religion holding them back from it? While in no way disagreeing with Wesley's judgement that he felt the need to know God in a direct way is a gift and a second blessing, it will probably clarify the ambiguities that are involved by considering it as a second conversion.

From seed to fruit

Propagation of entheism or novalism is in one sense a completely new challenge, calling for new structures and praxis but, on the other hand, history provides us with many valuable examples of how religious innovations developed and, even more valuable, why they failed. Four instances will be looked at below, but this is by no means an exclusive list. Had space allowed, it would have been useful to have included Islam, which provides valuable lessons, both positive and negative.

The first example of how new religious movements organize for growth is Christianity itself. It began with one man, Paul, preaching his new religion of salvation and eternal life and with those whom he convinced arranging themselves in small groups which met in each others' houses. Rather, perhaps, they met in the house of a member who was fortunate enough to have the required space and which thus became a microcosmic church. Paul was able to visit these gatherings until the numbers of Christians and their geographical spread grew too large, and he had to communicate with the emerging macro-church through writing letters, which were to become the foundational documents of the new religion. In time the house churches were to organize themselves in larger groupings, culminating in a structure of dioceses, each headed by a supervisor, which was the original meaning of the word *bishop*. This was a straightforward borrowing from political structure, the diocese being the administrative unit of the Roman Empire. As soon as the house churches were superseded by buildings specially designed as meeting places, Christians became a recognisable group, it was accorded legal status as a *collegium*, much as limited companies and building societies in the UK were given legal status in the 19th century. After the Protestant Reformation there were critical changes in church government and in the way that church space was organised, with architectural innovation answering to new needs. Most obviously, the stone altar on which the sacrifice of the Mass was offered and which was the focal point of the physical church was replaced with the pulpit, where the life-giving word of God was expounded, and with a table for re-enactment of the Eucharistic meal. The elaborate and sensuous liturgy of the Mass, enacted by a richly robed priest, was in general replaced with a more Spartan service, sometimes referred to rather flippantly as "a hymn and sermon sandwich".

After the Council of Nicaea in 325 Christianity spread within the Roman Empire mostly as an overlay on the civil structure, with authority centralised in Rome and bishoprics established in large centres of population. As the empire decayed and fell apart after the Barbarian invasions, the gospel message was taken beyond the old imperial boundaries by Celtic missionaries, who undertook the conversion of the German tribes of northern Europe. It was a most remarkable historical phenomenon, how a few hundred monks, mostly from Ireland and the Celtic areas of Britain, gave up their lives, often literally, to announce the good news, driven by the need to propagate what they clearly understood as a new hope for humanity. For them the gospel really was good news which they felt compelled to spread. Many gave their lives in the cause, for many of their hearers were not willing to abandon their familiar pagan gods and the unifying narrative of the Norse sagas. Boniface (675-754), today the patron saint of Germany, was among those killed, along with fifty two companions, for disturbing the status quo. It is a fascinating story, well told in Thomas Cahill's *How the Irish Saved Civilization*, whose seriousness is belied by its rather quirky title. Of particular note is a map showing the astonishing number of present day cities that either began or achieved prominence as monastic centres, among them Vienna, Strasbourg and Cologne [4], initiated by this small band of dedicated men. It cannot be too strongly emphasized that these "wild geese" left their homeland driven by the need to give to others a new world view and a new vision of humanity that they were intensely aware had been given to them. They lived in a world of new light surrounded by the darkness of the old, and this is surely significant today when so many feel a new darkness is descending over the world.

A third example of how religious structures emerge to meet the needs of the time is the Benedictine revolution, which began most inauspiciously with one man, Benedict of Nursia (480-543), fleeing from the corruption of Roman society to become a hermit. Quite unintentionally, Benedict gathered around him a growing number of men who wished to take him as their spiritual mentor and from this small seed was to grow almost an alternative church, until eventually its size and power led to corruption and decay. At its peak there were thousands of Benedictine houses in Europe, great and small, for both men and women, and the "Rule of St Benedict" was the most popular book in Europe after the Bible. They were set up specifically as "schools of the Lord's service" and also for personal development, *conversio morum*, in the words of the Rule. The nearest translation into English is "change of behaviour" or "change in way of life" and it is interesting to compare this with St Paul's *metanoia*, which is specifically "change in consciousness". Benedictine monasteries and priories were particularly numerous in Britain, until wiped out at a stroke by Henry VIII to seize their wealth and lands. Their remains, the "bare ruin'd choirs", as Shakespeare poignantly called them, are a melancholy monument to a great religious idealism. The rise and fall of Benedictinism is a most interesting cultural phenomenon for many reasons, but for present purposes the most important was that during the Dark Ages and for a thousand years Benedictine houses were islands of learning and civilisation. As against Celtic monks, who felt called to travel and spread the word, Benedictines took a vow of stability, committing them to stay in their home monastery. They were innovative agriculturalists, self-sustaining economically, had an unofficial social welfare system and were centres of learning, and islands of light in the gloom of the Dark Ages. Until the emergence of the first universities in the West in the 12th century, monastic schools were the only places of learning and for a thousand years, until printing was invented, monasteries provided an essential service to society by copying and distributing manuscripts, not least the works of the ancient Greek philosophers. It is no exaggeration to say that they constituted a publishing industry, and came to see this as a major function. The eminent historian David Knowles, in fact, marks the invention of printing in 1450 as the tipping point in their decline, when they lost their main social value [5]. Although the monastery and convent of their nature are set apart from society, there was almost always an interface, and it was usual for kings and nobles to send their sons to be educated in monastic schools. All in all, it may be said that Benedictinism played a critical part in seeing Christianity through the Dark Ages and shaping both the ideal and reality of Europe. This is recognized by the fact that Benedict was adopted as the patron saint of the European Community. There is something protean in the Benedictine concept of self-sustaining spiritual communities, deliberately set apart from society with all its cares and temptations but with a permeable boundary that enabled it to enrich society at the same time.

The fourth example chosen to illustrate how a religious ideal starts and propagates is the Quaker movement, which has its origins in isolated groups of self-identified "seekers" who emerged in England in the early 17th century, disillusioned with the religious and political institutions of the day. The religiously inclined separated out as "The Religious Society of Friends", largely under the influence of George Fox (1624-1691), who preached a return to basic Christian values but emphasized "that of God in all men" and the highly controversial ideal of "the priesthood of all believers". "Quakers" was at first a derogatory nickname which has stuck, ridiculing the fact that they often trembled under religious emotion. Rejecting the established church and without ordained ministers, their form of worship was stripped down to a long period of silence broken by vocal interjections from anyone present who felt moved by the Spirit to offer ministry. Fox wrote of a conversion experience, which might be compared to Paul's conversion on the Damascus road, after which everything changed and, as he recorded in his Journal, "All things were new and all the creation gave unto me another smell than before, beyond what words can utter." Without doubt this refers to the psychological effect of moving from a me-centred to a God-centred understanding of life. From a historical view perspective, the Quakers' most important contributions to religion were the replacement of liturgical worship with a period of silence and of the hierarchical authoritarian structure of traditional Christianity with a new democratic form of organisation. How far both innovations are now calling for a fresh look is a point to consider, for arteries harden as a movement develops into an institution and tradition becomes a subtle drag on fresh thinking and new insight. Quakerism is in rapid decline, particularly perhaps in Britain, where it no longer considers itself a specifically Christian body. The number of members is dropping almost exponentially and small meeting houses are closing down almost every month. While this can be put down to the rise of secularism as a quasi-religion, a major cause without doubt is the same lack of credibility in the

Judaeo-Christian narrative that is resulting in the wholesale closure of Christian churches.

Looking into the future

If entheism is not to remain merely an interesting theological speculation, those who wish to explore its potential must eventually come together to give it a corporate form of some kind. All four of the examples of religious development above provide valuable lessons for a nascent religious movement and while it is not within the remit of this short book to venture very far into this territory, it would be of value to point out some of them. The world has change radically since Christianity first appeared and nowhere so radically as in social structures and in communication. In both we are witnessing and taking part in revolutions whose final forms will not be known until they have run their course. In such uncertain times it is natural to look for guidance to authorities and recognized "opinion formers", but the obvious danger here is that they will be authorities in what is now passing away and they could easily be the worst possible guides for this reason. It will be natural to such experts to look backward, not forward. The instinctive reaction of most people to such a theological revolution as entheism here presented will be to look to church leaders and few of these are visionaries. They hold their position because they have been trusted to maintain present structures and practices. Their guiding principles are an inheritance from the past and nowhere so much as in the concept of leadership, which in the episcopalian type of church is modelled on the shepherd and the flock of dependent sheep and on a self-perpetuating and largely unelected priestly authority. Scripture provides a semblance of justification for this, since Jesus described himself as "the good shepherd" (John 10:1-18) and this kind of top-down and extreme dependency structure must of necessity be the norm when most people are illiterate or poorly informed. A new concept of religious leadership will be called for in a more literate and democratic society, as well as new structures of authority and learning. Mutual help and self-learning will assume a much greater importance in a modern day religion based single-mindedly on self-transformation. A new type of teacher can be foreseen emerging from those who are themselves on the path but can offer guidance to others less advanced or less spiritually gifted. Paradoxical as it may seem, the new leaders will be those who are most acutely aware that they themselves are, and always will be, learners. A richly embroidered cloak, imposing tall hat and mace of office are totally inappropriate symbols of the kind of spiritual leadership for which the world is now calling.

The conceptualised new religion cannot develop within a structure of gurus and devotees but only of co-learners and co-teachers. Together they will form a community extended in geographical space, joined together globally by communication technology and closely bound locally by new kinds of social structure, modelled in part on past historical experiments such as the Hutterites, Mennonites and Amish, as well as on the monastic ideal, as discussed briefly above. These will be communities in which individualism is cherished, in which self-learning and self-discipline will combine with mutual support and guidance, and which interface with the world at large and respond to social needs. Once Christians were committed quite specifically to such social services as "to visit the sick and imprisoned and bury the dead" in what were called "works of mercy". The love and sense of mutual dependence which energized early Christian communities are as essential a requirement now as then. While the welfare state has taken over most of society's fundamental needs, it is increasingly unable to fulfil them, as taxation revenue diminishes and is diverted to other priorities, not least feeding the military-industrial complex against which President Eisenhower warned against in his farewell address in 1961. Detail projections would not be appropriate here, but one exception should be made in drawing attention to the demographic crisis now becoming apparent in the Western world. We are becoming aware of great hidden suffering and deprivation in the lives of many old people whose need for care and social contact is not met by social services and realistically calls for a re-imagination of the kind of service that they need. This could well be a particular "work of mercy" undertaken in religious renewal.

In our individualistic age the need for unselfish service calls for particular emphasis. In a true religious community we are to be, as St Paul described it,

servants to one another in love (Gal. 5:13-15)

This ideal of mutual service runs throughout the documents of the early Christian church, and to quote one more example:

Above all, hold unfailingly your love for one another, since love covers a multitude of sins. Practice hospitality ungrudgingly to one another. As each has received a gift, employ it for one another. (1 Peter 4:7-11)

Notes and References

1. J. Krishnamurti, *The Nature of the New Mind*. Chennai: Krishnamurti Foundation, 2001. p. 223.
2. George Fox, for instance, advised the young William Penn, wavering between religious commitment and aristocratic fashion, "Wear thy sword as long as thou canst." Abbot John Chapman, similarly, having told a correspondent that silent prayer was the best kind, then advised her not to strive for it but to "pray with words as long as you can."
3. Dom John Chapman, *Spiritual Letters*. London: Sheed and Ward, 1935 (reprinted 2003). pp. 113 ff. The most recent editor comments that Chapman "towers" above others as a practical guide to contemplative prayer. He asks the important questions. However, although he wrote in the early 20th century, his thought-world is thoroughly mediaeval and, for instance, he takes as historical the story of Adam the perfect man who fell from grace. Had he seen humanity in an evolutionary progression, many of his answers would come into clearer focus.
4. Thomas Cahill, *How the Irish Saved Civilization*. London: Hodder and Stoughton, 1995. p. 194.
5. A comprehensive picture of the development and importance of the Benedictine revolution can be found in David Knowles, *Christian Monasticism* (NY: Mcraw-Hill, 1972 [1969] and in *The Benedictines* (Eugene: OR, Wipf & Stock, 2009 [Macmillan 1930].